What Health Care Professionals Say About *Babywise II*

As an Asia- and America-trained pediatrician, I know that the principles in *Babywise II* work cross-culturally.... This book helps parents to be proactive in their training, giving them a basic plan of action so they can direct their children to succeed in the moral and academic disciplines of life. From experience with my two sons and the results of my patients, I enthusiastically recommend the *Babywise* books as a must-read for parents.

Saphry-May Liauw, M.D., M.S. (Pharm)
Jakarta, Indonesia

As a practicing pediatric neurologist, husband, and father, I fully endorse and highly recommend *Babywise II*. The principles found in this book—highly researched, immensely and universally applicable—are life-changing for families.

In my practice of pediatric neurology, the foundational principles and the practical recommendations [found in *Babywise II*] have been useful to many parents who have sought my expertise in working with problems in behavior, development, attention, learning, discipline, and sleep. If *Babywise II* principles were widely applied in the early months and years as they should be, I would see far fewer patients over the age of two for problems in these areas.

Virtually all of the books available on child development, behavior management, attentional disorders, and so on, fall far short when compared to the wisdom, practicality, and confidence offered in this volume.

Robert P. Turner, M.D.
Richmond, Virginia

As a *Babywise* pediatrician, every newborn baby is a challenge and excitement to me, because I know I can help them with their moral behaviors as well as their physical well-being. *Babywise II* enables me to contribute to t`_____ ___ _____ _f children, which is much needed in our _____ _____ _____ effective book is an invaluable asset to my practice, since no other medical textbook strikes so deeply into the basic needs of life.

Peter Y. S. Kim, M.D.
Valencia, California

Finally, a parenting guide that is practical, makes sense and works! *Babywise II* provides today's parents with the up-to-date parenting strategies needed for the 90s. As a pediatric professional, I enthusiastically recommend this book as a vital road map for the pre-toddler months.

Penn Laird, M.D.
Pediatric Cardiologist
Dallas, Texas

ON BECOMING

BABY WISE

BOOK TWO

Parenting Your Pre-Toddler
Five to Fifteen Months

■

GARY EZZO AND
ROBERT BUCKNAM, M. D.

MULTNOMAH BOOKS

BABYWISE II: PARENTING YOUR PRETODDLER,
FIVE TO FIFTEEN MONTHS

published by Multnomah Books
a part of the Questar publishing family

© 1995 by Gary Ezzo and Robert Bucknam, M.D.

International Standard Book Number: 0-88070-807-7

Edited by Stephen T. Barclift

Designed by David Carlson

Photo by FPG International/Jill Sabella ©1994

Printed in the United States of America

For information:
QUESTAR PUBLISHERS, INC.
POST OFFICE BOX 1720
SISTERS, OREGON 97759

97 98 99 00 01 02 — 10 9 8 7 6 5

To

Ashley, Whitney, Kara, Katelynn,

and Robert Joseph (R.J.)

ACKNOWLEDGMENTS

We are grateful for the valued assistance of many co-workers, including Tim and Patricia Lentz, Scott and Theresa McLeod, David and Cynthia Iglesias, Tiana Wendelburg, and Sharon Augustson. All of them contributed in important ways to the preparation of this text.

We also are grateful to Connie Lamoureux for her help with the language development material found in Appendix A, and to Nancy Martin and sketch artist Yvonne Wilber for their contributions to the section on sign language training (Appendix B).

Finally, a special thanks goes to our friends and teaching colleagues: Eric and Julie Abel, and Gary and Robyn Vander Weide. Their collective wisdom and applied experience gives this book its practical foundation.

CONTENTS

FOREWORD

As a pediatrician, I am concerned about healthy children. "Healthy" means more than just positive ear, nose, and throat examinations. Healthy growth includes physical, moral, and academic fitness. *Babywise II* focuses on each of these categories.

Parenting a pretoddler arouses many different emotions—in the parents and the child. Love, joy, peace, contentment, and confidence are easily matched by the emotions of frustration, disappointment, and discouragement (and on some days, despair). Parenting to achieve all the right emotions is not the purpose of child-training—yet many parents believe it is. For them, childrearing is reduced to avoidance of all negative emotions and pursuit of positive ones. For this reason, right and wrong training is measured by how parents think their child *feels,* rather than by the end product—their child's *behavior.* The feelings of parent and child become the basis of nurturing. If the child feels happy, the parent is satisfied. If the child feels sad, then the parent works to create an environment that will eliminate his or her sadness. That approach is not healthy for children, families, or society in general.

The ultimate objective of parenting in a free society is a moral one. The duty of every parent is to raise a morally responsible child who will grow up to be a morally responsible adult. Such an important task shouldn't be put off until a child is "mature enough to understand." The job of every parent is to raise a child who at each phase of growth is a blessing, not only to the parents, but to everyone else the child comes in contact with.

We base this book on a moral model of child development, not a psychological one. The moral training of a child is the foundation of his or her upbringing (yes, even in the pretoddler phase), the result being a child who is healthy, happy, and relationally secure throughout life.

9

Moral training is a priority discipline. The success achieved in all the major disciplines of life (for example, skills development, academic achievement, and forming healthy interpersonal relationships), is tied to and dependent on the quality of moral training. Children who have internal self-control and mastery of the "please and thank you's" of life also have the self-control that will help them secure a healthy academic and relational life. The moral self-control that keeps a child sitting in a highchair without fighting with mom is the same self-control that will later keep him at a desk with a book in his hand. The battle for right highchair manners is moral, not academic. In fact, most of what parents do by way of training in the early months and years serves a broader moral purpose.

Why, then, is moral training important? When you rightly train the heart of a child, you lay down a solid foundation for the other disciplines of life. And the results show. Parents tell me that, not only are they wonderfully pleased with the results of utilizing the principles found in this book, their friends and relatives are *amazed* at the accomplishments of those parents' pretoddlers. *Babywise* laid down the right foundation; *Babywise II* provides the right structure for creating a suitable learning environment for advancing any child in the crucial disciplines of life.

To experience the right emotions in parenting, right training is a prerequisite. *Babywise II* will help you accomplish that objective.

Robert Bucknam, M.D.

INTRODUCTION

It's reality-check time! You are at least five months into your tour of parenting duty by now. The complexity of child-training has begun to come into focus. You have learned that as your baby matures, both constant and variable factors continually influence his or her development. But now, as the baby moves into the pretoddler phase, the variables of growth begin to play a more dominant role. How will you respond to those variables? Certainly not by abandoning that which has brought you so much success—your baby's routine. No, you will want to preserve the order and structure that brings security to your baby and stability to your home.

You must now become *principle-minded*, learning how to rightly respond to the emerging variables of your pretoddler's life. You need to know what to expect, when to expect it, and at what ages different patterns of behavior will normally emerge. Knowing the progressive nature of growth and development enables you as a parent to set standards of expected behavior, and provides the guidance needed to help your child reach your behavioral goals.

What behaviors can and should you expect from your pretoddler? Feeding time for your pretoddler, for example, is now more than a response controlled by a sucking reflex. For the pretoddler, mealtime is part of a very complex, conscious interaction between what the child does and what his parents expect him to do. Right and wrong conduct will be encouraged, discouraged, and guided when necessary. In fact, right and wrong patterns of behavior will now be part of your baby's entire day. That's why feeding time, waketime, and bedtime provide wonderful opportunities for training.

This book will emphasize the importance of establishing learning patterns—right learning patterns. Those patterns form learning structures that assist the child throughout his or her early development. Just as cartilage strengthens and turns into bone, so also learning patterns develop and form the basis of future moral and academic learning. Therefore, the first patterns established need to be right patterns. Researchers and educators agree that growth and development take place in stages, with new experiences building upon previous ones. *Babywise II* is designed to assist parents in establishing the right patterns of learning for their child, providing the necessary framework for the development, over time, of many crucial life skills.

The practical nature of *Babywise II* allows any parent of a pre-toddler to take advantage of the information provided. But those best served are the graduates of our first book, *Babywise*. In *Babywise*, we introduced the foundational principles that *Babywise II* is built upon, including routine feedings, naps, and the establishment of healthy nighttime sleep. (A baby usually can learn to sleep through the night within the first six to eight weeks of life.) We encourage parents not familiar with the concepts of *Babywise* to first become acquainted with them before moving forward with *Babywise II*.

As was true with *Babywise*, we can give you trustworthy principles, but not every possible application. As you read, it is vital that you think in terms of *principle*. Once armed with a principle, you can apply that principle in a way that makes sense in your baby's specific situation.

The next ten months are critical. The stakes are high. From this point forward, you are going after the heart of your child. Many parents place a greater emphasis on a child's psychological health than on his or her moral health. Parental preoccupation with psychological nurturing is not the medicine for the problem; too often, such preoccupation is the *problem itself*, producing emotionally fragile children. Moral health, with an emphasis on heart training, is the medicine preventing emotional deficiencies. *Babywise II* will advance that cause for you.

In the back of this book we have added three appendices: Appendix A—"Child Language Development"; Appendix B—"Teach

Your Child to Sign"; and Appendix C—"Thoughts on Potty Training."
There is much helpful, totally practical information in these appendices; read them at your leisure.

Many rewarding experiences are ahead for you. Happy pretoddler parenting!

Gary Ezzo

Chapter One

Back to the Basics

*I*n *Babywise,* we stressed the importance of establishing a right mind-set for parenting. In *Babywise II,* we will stress the importance of maintaining that mind-set as your baby approaches his or her first birthday. A child's personality is shaped by forces present in the early years. Parents are a young child's whole world—and they are the greatest influence in the child's life. Therefore, before moving forward with this book, we must first return to some of the foundational principles that brought you to your first level of success. They include 1) *understanding the priority of marriage,* 2) *recognizing the dangers of child-centered parenting,* and 3) *knowing how to avoid extremism in the parenting process.* Let's review the basics.

THE PRIORITY OF MARRIAGE

Marriage represents a special bond between two people that is matched by no other relationship. At least that was the original idea. Marriage is unique—totally without parallel. It transcends all other relationships. How truly amazing it is! Here's an important outcome of making the most of marriage: *Great marriages produce great parents.*

A healthy husband-wife relationship is essential to the emotional health of children in the home. When there is harmony in the marriage, there is stability within the family. A strong marriage provides a haven of security for children as they grow in the nurturing process. Healthy, loving marriages create a sense of certainty for children. When a child observes the special friendship and emotional togetherness of his parents, he or she is more secure simply because it isn't necessary to question the legitimacy of the parents' commitment to one another.

Children possess an amazing type of "radar" that hones in on parental conflict. When a child perceives more weakness than strength in his or her parents' relationship, a low-level anxiety results, ultimately putting a strain on every other learning discipline the child experiences. A child knows intuitively, just as his or her own parents knew when growing up, that if something happens to mom and dad, the child's whole world will collapse. If the parents' relationship is in question in the mind of a child, that child will live his life on the brink of collapse.

When the marital relationship is made beautiful, what impressionable child would not want to be part of the family? When two are mysteriously and beautifully united in marriage, what child would not seek the comforts of that togetherness? The best years of parenting will flow out of the best years of marriage. Protect your marriage!

DANGERS OF CHILD-CENTERED PARENTING

Child-centered parenting threatens successful family life. Listed below are five dangers associated with this style of family government.

1. *Child-centered parenting attacks the husband-wife relationship by reducing its practical significance.* In marriage, neither men nor women can lose themselves; marriage forces revelation. We are revealed for what we are. Child-centered parenting, however, wrongly authorizes one or the other in the partnership to pull away—to make room for the child, who now is the focus of the home. We then become less revealed to our spouse, thus less honest about who we are. Attempting to avoid the truth about ourselves, we conveniently find in the name of fatherhood or motherhood a more pleasing image. Whenever we pull away from marriage, no matter how seemingly noble the reason, we leave our source of accountability—our mate. Your children deserve the best from the two of you.

2. *Child-centered parenting reverses the natural process of moral development by prematurely creating within a child a false sense of self-reliance.* The child becomes, in his own thinking, self-sufficient prior to the establishment of necessary self-control. That happens because the child-centered parenting philosophy grants freedoms beyond the child's ability to manage those freedoms. Self-reliance apart from self-discipline is a destructive influence on young children.

3. *Child-centered parenting fosters family independence, not family*

interdependence. Children who perceive themselves to be the center of the family universe too often grow into selfish independence. Family independence (rather than family interdependence) becomes a way of life—a lonely one. Independence robs a child of the opportunity to invest in relationships. Where there is no relational investment, there is no reason for family loyalty. Other people (parents, siblings, and peers) matter only to the extent that advantages are gained by maintaining relationships. What the child can get out of relationships, rather than what he or she can give, forms the basis of the child's loyalty. Child-centered parenting fosters that conclusion.

4. *Child-centered parenting magnifies the conflict between the natural way of the child and his or her need for moral conformity.* Child-centered parenting creates propensities toward negative behavior that will either force the parent and child into an adversarial relationship or force parents to abandon any reasonable standard of moral accountability.

5. *Child-centered parenting is reactive, not proactive.* Reacting to crises in a child's life is inferior to preventing them.

Now that your baby is here, you can see how easily child-centered parenting can creep into your day. If you put *Babywise* principles into practice, you avoided *demand feeding,* but were you equally as successful at avoiding *parental attention on demand,* which is the precursor to child-centered parenting? The infant's total dependence on parental care heightens the gratification of the parenting experience. Fortunately, parents can avoid both outcomes. You can meet all your baby's physical and emotional needs and not be child-centered.

Here are a few reminders from *Babywise* that can help you maintain the balance.

1. *Remind yourself that life does not stop once you have a baby.* Life may slow down for a few weeks, but it doesn't stop completely. When you become a mother, you don't stop being a daughter, a sister, a friend, and most importantly, a wife. Those relationships were important to you before the baby arrived. Be sure to maintain them afterward.

2. *If you had a weekly date night with your spouse before the baby was born, continue that practice, letting friends or relatives watch your baby.* If you did not date on a regular basis, start now. Your date doesn't have to be expensive or a late night out. And keep this in mind, too: A child doesn't suffer from what many refer to as "separation anxiety" when mom is out with dad rather than remaining at home constantly with the baby. As noted above, the marriage relationship is the starting point of security for children.

3. *Don't give up those special gestures for each other that characterized your marriage before you had a child.* If there was a favorite activity you both enjoyed previously, plan it into your schedule. If a husband brings home a gift for the baby, he should also give flowers to his wife. The idea here is basic—continue to make those loving gestures that marked your relationship as special and keep it special.

4. *Practice couch time.* When the workday is over, take fifteen minutes and sit on the couch together as a couple. This should take place when your children are awake, not after they go to bed. Explain to your children the importance of having no

unnecessary interruptions, because this is a special time for the two of you. Explain that Dad will play afterward, but Mom has his full attention right now—because she's special to him. Couch time provides a visual sense of your togetherness. In this tangible way, children can measure their mom and dad's love relationship and have that inner need satisfied. In addition, couch time provides a predictable forum for a couple to share their relational needs with each other.

5. *Invite friends over for a meal or an evening of companionship.* Focusing on hospitality is a healthy distraction from the rigors of childrearing. It obligates you to plan your child's day around serving other people, rather than just your child.

6. *Don't make the mistake of keeping information from your spouse, either by intent or neglect.* Parenting is a "team sport." It maximizes your collective insights so you can understand your children better and train them properly. As the primary caregiver, mom must consider it her duty to keep dad updated on what she is observing.

If you desire excellence in parenting, work continually at protecting your marriage. A right perspective about the significance of that relationship is the starting point for healthy parent-child relationships.

PARENTING EXTREMISM AND CONTEXT

As we stated in *Babywise*, it's important that you avoid the extremes of parenting. This will be true throughout your childrearing years. Mothers and fathers who parent in the extremes create problems when they elevate their personal parenting philosophy above what is best for the child at any given moment. That is, they elevate the rule of behavior above the principle the rule represents. This form of extreme parenting is appropriately labeled *legalism*.

We've all heard the phrase, "Let's keep things in context." The most notable aspect of a legalist is that he or she rejects context. Responding to the context—the unique set of circumstances defining a situation—doesn't mean suspending the principles of *Babywise*. Rather, you can focus on the right response in the short-term, without compromising your long-term objectives.

There will be times when the context of a situation will dictate a temporary suspension of some general guidelines. As a parent, you are endowed with experience, wisdom, and common sense. Trust those attributes first, not your emotions at a particular moment or the rigidity of the clock. When special situations arise, allow context to guide you. The following are a couple of examples of how and when this should occur.

1. You are on an airplane and your six-month-old begins to fuss loudly. You last fed him only two hours earlier. What should you do? If neither you nor a toy can satisfy your son, consider offering a feeding. The context and ethics involved require that you not let your baby's routine disturb the flight for everyone else. Failing to act will bring stress both to you and to the rest of the passengers. Although you normally wouldn't feed him so soon after his last feeding, the context of the situation dictates that you temporarily suspend your normal routine. When you arrive at your destination, resume your basic routine. (For more information on traveling with your baby, please see chapter 7.)

2. You and your ten-month-old daughter are staying overnight in the home of a friend. She usually sleeps through the night, but this night she wakes at 3:00 A.M. What is the morally correct action to take? Pacify the child and help her return to sleep. Yes, at home she may fall back to sleep in five minutes with a little bit of fussing or crying, but you're not at home—you are a guest in someone else's home, and your child is disturbing the sleep of others. When you return home, get back to your basic routine and your child will follow suit.

Most of your day will be routine and predictable. But there will be times when you need to be more flexible due to unusual circumstances. Your life will be less tense if you consider the context of each situation and respond appropriately for the benefit of everyone.

SUMMARY

Man is by nature a social creature—both in the broader context of the community in which he lives his public life and in the narrower context of the intimacy of his private world. Man needs someone with whom he can share life, be complete, and have emotional, physical, and spiritual intimacy. All this adds up to marriage and the need to protect it. Neither child-centered parenting nor legalism serve your marriage or your children. They are damaging practices which must be avoided, for the benefit of your family life and your children.

QUESTIONS FOR REVIEW

1. What happens when a child perceives more weakness than strength in his or her parents' relationship? *they become anxious; putting strain on learning.*

2. How does child-centered parenting reverse the natural process of moral development? Explain. *it makes them think they are self-sufficient no self-control/self-discipline*

3. Why is couch time so important? *it provides a visual togetherness for your children. provides a forum for couples to share their needs w/ each other.*

4. What do parenting extremists create? *problems for what is best for the child @ any given moment.*

5. What does a legalist reject? Explain. *Context. Circumstances defining a situation. Focus on right response in short-term, w/o comprimising long-term objectives.*

Chapter Two

Moral
Foundations

hroughout your baby's first year of life, two processes dominate: growth and learning. These processes are interdependent, but not interchangeable. *Growth* refers to the biological changes and maturation taking place; *learning* pertains to the mental processes, which include moral training and development. With both growth and learning, changes in your child are progressive—each stage of development depends on, and builds upon, successful completion of the previous stage.

FACTORS OF GROWTH

Every species, whether animal or human, follows a pattern of development unique to that species. In postnatal development, infants demonstrate two growth patterns: vertical, from head down to feet; and horizontal, from the central axis of the body toward the extremities.

Vertical development takes place in a *descending* manner—from top to toe. This means that advancements in structure and function come first to a child's head region, then to the child's trunk (body), and, finally, to the legs and feet. Here is the typical progression: Your baby first lifts his or her head, bobbing it a little, and then lets it fall back to the mattress. Next, the child begins to hold the head upright as a result of developing neck and chest muscles. By the age of twenty weeks, he or she develops control over the muscles of the eyes, head, and shoulders, but the baby's trunk is still so limp that the child has to be propped up or strapped in a chair in order to maintain a sitting position. Your baby will make good use of his or her arms and hands in reaching and grasping before using the legs. Eventually, your child will motor around by creeping and then crawling, followed by walking, running, jumping, and skipping.

Horizontal development proceeds from simple to complex. Growth in the prenatal state starts with the head region and descends to the trunk. Those regions are well developed before the arms and legs begin to grow. Gradually, the arms lengthen, followed by the development of hands and fingers. Functionally, in the postnatal state a baby will use his or her chest muscles first, then the arms, and then hands. Your baby will use his or her hands as a unit before being able to control the movements of fingers. *Order* is the operative word for biological maturation—physical growth always occurs in an orderly, predictable way.

FACTORS OF LEARNING

Whereas biological maturation refers to changes in physical capabilities that result from genetic cues, learning signifies changes resulting from interaction with one's *environment;* for the most part, learning is brought about by parental influence and instruction. Like adults, children interpret new experiences in relationship to knowledge formerly acquired. That means learning is progressive, and a child only gains understanding when new information has meaning in relationship to previous experiences. Routine and orderly transition at each stage of the child's development aid the marriage between new information and a child's understanding.

Allowing a child to progress in an orderly manner into his or her new and expanding world greatly enhances learning. It is the gradual assimilation of many perceptions that gives rise to the formation of ideas. The child who can associate right meanings with new experiences is far more advanced in his or her understanding than the child who must associate a new meaning with an old situation that stands in need of correction. Since learning comes in progressive stages, training should take place in the same way, occurring hand-in-hand with progressions in learning. For this reason, parents need to provide their child with a learning environment that matches information with understanding.

There are many factors that influence learning, both positively and negatively. The child's temperament, the presence or absence of siblings, parental resolve, the purpose for training, the method of instruction, and reinforcement are some of the more obvious ones. Generally speaking, there are three categories of learning: basic skills, academics, and moral development. Let's take a look at each one.

Skills

Not all behavior is moral in nature. Some actions are morally neutral—such as those related to basic skills. One of the most important and most rapid areas of development during the early years of a child's life is the development of motor skills. Learning to use a spoon, walk, swim, tie a shoelace, ride a bike, kick a ball, and climb a rope are *amoral*—neither moral nor immoral—stage-acquired activities. They are skills associated to a large extent with the child's environment, opportunities to learn, and his or her motivation to do so. From the helpless state of infancy, skills-development begins and moves forward. Most children learn these feats in progressive stages. For example, when a toddler throws a ball, he or she uses the whole body. As coordination develops, the child will throw the ball using only the arm.

Skills, talents, and giftedness are not the same, by the way. Skills—such as learning to walk, coloring within the lines, riding a bike, learning to swim, and throwing a ball—are basic to all human beings. Natural talents differ from skills in that they are discriminatory—some people have a particular talent, others don't. All of us have talents, but not necessarily the *same* talents. Giftedness is a talent magnified. Many musicians are naturally talented, but Mozart was *gifted.*

Academic Learning

Academic learning is the accumulation of data and the ability to apply logic—reasoning skills—to given situations. Academic learning, much like physical development, moves from general to specific and is progressive. We teach our children the alphabet so they can learn to put letters together to form words, then read those words. They first learn to count—1, 2, 3, 4, 5; but it will be a while before they realize that those numbers also can represent 12,345. Children first learn about trees in general, then begin to distinguish, for example, pine from oak. Eventually, they will learn to identify the different varieties of pine trees.

Moral Development

While academic training is important, it isn't more important than, nor mutually exclusive from, moral training. They both need to be taking place from infancy on. At birth, a child has no functioning conscience. By that we mean the child possesses no awareness of standards of right and wrong. From the start, parents should strive to raise a child who regulates his own behavior from within, in accordance with the rules of common ethics. Until the child internalizes healthy moral principles, parents are obligated to make value judgments and moral decisions on behalf of the child. In early parenting, this means that external pressure is necessary to bring about acceptable behavior, even though the child has no understanding of the reason for the behavior. The fact that a child has no moral understanding about why food shouldn't be intentionally dropped from his or her highchair doesn't mean we should hold back instructions and restrictions.

With adults, beliefs precede actions. But with children, the opposite is true—actions precede beliefs. This is why parents should insist on moral behavior long before their child is capable of understanding moral concepts. Children first learn how to act morally, and then they learn how to think morally. The two phases of moral training include: 1) *the development of moral behavior,* and 2) *the development of moral concepts.* Actions come first, understanding comes second. This book is concerned only with the importance of moral behavior.

MORAL AND SELF-CONTROL TRAINING

What constitutes moral behavior in pretoddlers? Probably more actions than you think. The fact that infants don't yet make moral choices doesn't mean moral behavior isn't taking place and moral training isn't required. It is! Developing healthy learning patterns is the child's first step toward moral understanding. Structure and your baby's basic routine enhance the establishment of those patterns. When a child is at peace with his basic environment, his learning potential increases and learning disorders are minimized. In contrast, infants reared by the immediate-gratification style of parenting—which has at its root the belief that the child's every need, whether real or perceived, must be dealt with instantly in order to fully satisfy the child—develop unhealthy learning patterns.

Timely gratification training leads to greater self-control in children, which then leads to longer attention spans and an advanced aptitude for academic and moral learning. The key term here is *self-control*. Self-control is a base virtue. That is, other virtues in an individual can't exist without it. Self-control influences kindness, gentleness, proper speech, and the ability to control negative emotions, as well as focusing skills, sitting skills, and many other behaviors. When you train your child to a right moral response, you simultaneously train him or her in self-control.

This is a major fork in the road in behavioral studies. Many theorists accept human reason as the basis of morality and focus on intellectual stimulation as a priority, ahead of moral development. However, we invite the reader to consider this opposing view: *Moral education not only should be a priority of early training, it is absolutely necessary for optimum intellectual achievement.*

Why is that true? Because self-control is not an academic discipline—it's a moral one. Sitting, focusing, and concentrating are also moral disciplines borrowed by the intellect to advance academic achievement. At nine months of age, my (Gary's) granddaughter Ashley, began to arch her back defiantly while sitting in the highchair. Her actions were moral, and her parents' response was moral—they worked to eliminate the behavior, and Ashley learned to sit still by eleven months of age. She was trained to indicate her desire for more food or to get down from her highchair by *signing* with her hands. (See Appendix B, "Teach Your Baby to Sign," for practical instruction in how to use this important training tool.) Because nine-month-old babies have some mental ability to communicate, but not the verbal skill, signing became the acceptable way for Ashley to communicate, rather than arching her back.

What was most significant about Ashley's training was not the signing itself, but the level of Ashley's self-control. The self-control she used to not arch her back and the self-control she used to accurately communicate her wishes were one and the same. No training in moral self-control is ever isolated. The self-control needed to sit, think, and choose a better way to communicate is the same self-control that will safeguard the child through life. Such self-control is the product of moral training and not the result of doing flash cards, playing educational games, or learning baby math. There was a moral reason for Ashley to learn self-control, even though she was not aware of that reason.

Waiting until a child is five years old is much too late to start working on the skills of sitting, focusing, and concentrating. These are moral developmental skills, not stage-acquired activities. They are skills that depend on orderly structure from the earliest days of life. Even now, during your baby's first year of life, you are laying the foundations for future development. Healthy moral development pays academic dividends.

Can parents alter their child's intelligence quotient (IQ)? No. Can they maximize or limit it? Yes. We maintain this perspective because we have consistently found that parents who rejected structure in the early years and did nothing to correct a lack of structure in the toddler years, had actually slowed and in many cases corrupted the process of moral and intellectual development. That's why *Babywise II* focuses on the heart of the child—that portion of our humanity from which the issues of life flow. Parents who work on the heart will ultimately train the whole child. Those who work exclusively on the intellect will, at best, raise a smart but morally weak child.

PARENTING INSIDE THE FUNNEL

Please examine the growth funnel diagram on page 33. The long stem of the funnel represents the early stages of parenting, while the wider portion represents a child's growth, maturing process, and gradual attainment of freedoms. Here's how this works: As the child grows up through the stem, freedoms are earned to the extent that the child demonstrates responsible behavior.

A common mistake parents sometimes make is to *parent outside the funnel* in the pretoddler months. By "outside the funnel," we are referring to those times when parents allow behaviors that are neither age-appropriate nor in harmony with a child's moral and intellectual capabilities. To allow a seven-month-old baby freedoms appropriate

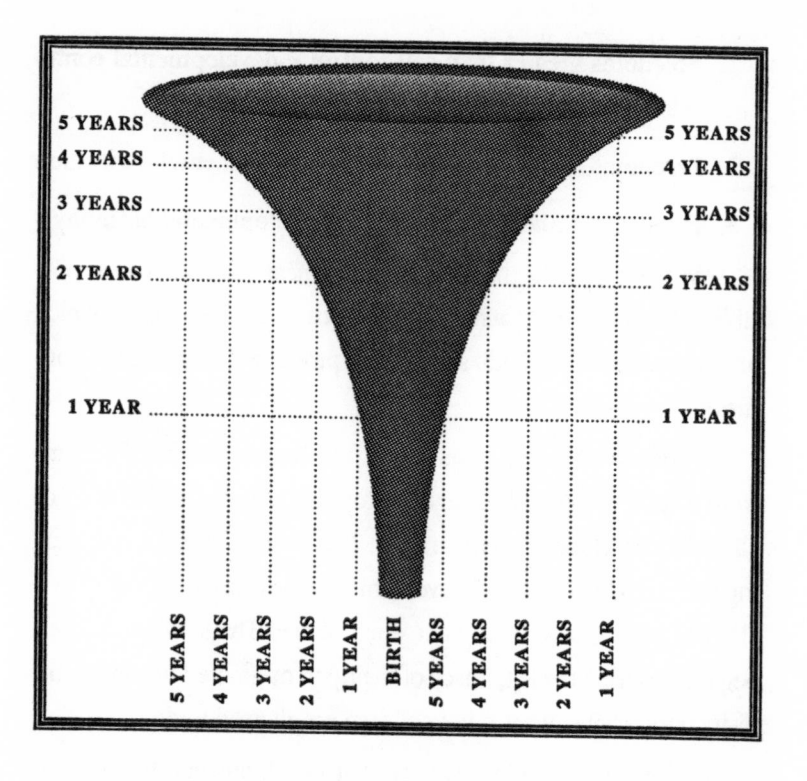

for a two-year-old, or a one-year-old freedoms suitable for a five-year-old, is to parent outside the funnel. Such freedoms don't facilitate healthy learning patterns.

Here is the heart of this matter: *Your desire for the developmental harmony of your child makes it necessary that you grant freedoms to the child only after he or she attains the age-appropriate level of self-control.* A freedom granted a child who is not guided by the amount of self-control necessary to handle that freedom ultimately leads the child to enslavement to his passions. When freedoms granted are greater or less than the child's self-control capacities, a state of developmental imbalance is created. Please consider the following basic equations:

1. **Freedoms greater than self-control = developmental confusion**

2. **Freedoms less than self-control = developmental frustration**

3. **Freedoms equal to self-control = developmental harmony**

We want to make these equations as meaningful for you as possible. The first one explains that freedoms granted to a child which are greater than the child's self-control produce developmental confusion.

Number two above refers to the fact that withholding freedoms from a child who possesses age-appropriate self-control will eventually foster developmental frustration. This usually doesn't occur during the pretoddler phase of development but typically shows up in a child of between five and eight years of age. That's when children begin measuring the legitimacy of their parent-granted freedoms and restrictions against what other children are allowed to do.

In the third equation, we see that developmental harmony is achieved when freedoms awarded a child are appropriate for his or her level of self-control. The following scenarios further illustrate these concepts.

Jim and Brenda Johnson were excited about the mobility of their crawling nine-month-old son, Joshua. Determined not to stifle his exploration, they imposed no limits on him. He had the freedom to touch and explore anything at will. But what happens when the Johnson family visits the home of friends or relatives, or goes shopping, and Joshua touches and perhaps handles everything in sight? How will they restrain him? How will he perceive those restraints? All of a sudden, limitations are placed on a behavior that had no previous limitations. That is more than confusing to a child—it creates an unnecessary adversarial conflict between the child and his or her parents. No child wants to give up territory once it has been gained.

The problem began when Joshua's parents failed to set age-appropriate boundaries during the early days of his mobility. Because of this lack of restraint, Joshua's mobility put him in an environment larger than he could manage. The excess freedom created too many new variables that he was not ready to handle. Jim and Brenda were parenting outside the funnel. They should have limited Joshua's field of exploration by setting appropriate boundaries, training him to respect those boundaries, and then allowing restraint to give way to freedom. Instead, they reversed the process, forcing freedom to give way to restraint, since Joshua was not able to rightly interact with his environment. Rather than move him gradually forward toward increased freedom, Joshua's parents had to move him *backward* toward restraint.

Certainly there will be times when you will recall a prematurely granted freedom because the child is not ready to handle the associated responsibilities. Recalling privileges should not be the norm in your parenting, however, but the exception. You can help yourself avoid reparenting by evaluating what you allow your child to play with or do.

For example, do you let your eight-month-old play with the television remote control? If yes, why? Does the child understand what it's used for, how it works, or why it's not a toy? When he or she begins to bang it on the coffee table, will you take it away? Or when the child picks up and begins to bang a similar unit on the neighbor's coffee table, how will you restrain him or her? What are you going to do when your child resists your taking possession of it? All of a sudden you are surrounded by variables that should never have become part of your baby's life. Letting your child play with the remote control is parenting outside the funnel. At this age of development, a remote control has no meaning or purpose. Why add a variable to your baby's life that will only need correction later? Allowing a child unlimited freedom of exploration is developmentally unwise and unhealthy. *Freedom is not the problem—the problem is the child's inability to handle the power of freedom.* It's worth keeping in mind that failure to correct a child today will lead to moral tyranny tomorrow.

Here is another example. Becky's parents found it amusing to watch her tear up old newspapers. She really enjoyed this seemingly harmless form of entertainment. But this situation, too, is of a type that can quickly get out of hand. For one thing, Becky's parents should have recognized the potential dangers involved: The sharp edges of paper, even newsprint, can cut tender skin; a child can swallow and choke on torn paper, or perhaps be poisoned by toxic ink that is ingested; and there is a chance the child might get ink in her eyes. Besides being dangerous, the fun of tearing paper can lead to the fun of tearing pages out of books—mom's, dad's, a sibling's, or the baby's own. Then what will the baby's parents do? Not only must they correct the behavior, but now the child has limited access to educational opportunities to be gained from her books. This, too, is an example of parenting outside the funnel. As in the case of the Johnson family, reparenting must take place.

To avoid reparenting, which usually produces less than satisfactory results, you should continually evaluate what you allow your child to do according to his or her age-level, understanding, and abilities. Are you giving the child inappropriate freedoms? Parent the constant factors and control the variables until the child has the moral capacity to handle the freedom those variables bring. Let's take another look at our third equation: Freedoms granted that are equal to a child's level of self-control equals developmental harmony. Harmony! What a beautiful word for a pretoddler's and toddler's world.

The word *harmony* means combining parts into a pleasing and orderly whole. That's exactly what parents should strive to do with their pretoddler. Take the three parts of your baby's day—feeding time, waketime, and naptime—and bring harmony to each one. Let's return to our earlier example of the remote control. The child who is offered an age-appropriate toy in place of the remote control will less likely need to have limitations placed on the use of the toy. By providing the appropriate toy, not only are you controlling the variables by offering the appropriate play item, but you are also limiting the need for constant correction. It is constant correction and placement of limitations that disrupts the child's world, leading to developmental confusion.

Are you giving your pretoddler inappropriate freedoms? The twelve-month-old who at nine months of age learned his boundaries and how to respond to his parents' voice limitations, can handle many more freedoms at home and away than the child who had the freedoms early but lost them because of uncontrollable behavior. Life for you and your baby will be much more manageable and pleasant when you parent within the funnel, allowing restraint to give way to freedoms.

SUMMARY

As a parent, you are obligated to produce a responsible human being, and that challenge should not be left up to chance. Accept the challenges of parenting, realizing that the process of training your child starts with you. Belonging to your family is not an option for your child, but a mandate. That means moral conformity is required. There are certain virtues worth acquiring, such as kindness, goodness, gentleness, charity, honesty, honor, and respect. Since these qualities are not naturally found in a child's life, they must be instilled and nurtured into his or her heart.

You are the governors of your child's life. Be proud of that fact. Don't shy away from your responsibility, though it is great. You are to govern until your child develops within his or her heart the self-control and moral precepts necessary for self-governance. Self-legislative freedoms come gradually: In an appropriate amount of time, your child will be allowed to advance from the playpen, to the backyard, to the neighborhood. As your child demonstrates age-responsible behavior and sound judgment, he or she will earn another level of freedom. This type of training results in a developmentally healthy child who is a joy to everyone.

QUESTIONS FOR REVIEW

1. Briefly describe the three categories of learning.

    a.

    b.

    c.

2. What are two phases of moral training?

3. Why is gaining self-control so important to a child?

4. Explain why moral education should not only be a priority of early training, but is absolutely necessary for optimum intellectual achievement.

5. How is the growth funnel analogy discussed in this chapter rightly used?

6. What is implied by the phrase "parenting outside the funnel"?

Chapter Three

Mealtime Activities

*I*n *Babywise*, we introduced the three primary activities of your baby's day—feeding time, waketime, and naptime. With age-appropriate modifications, those same activities continue through the toddler years. Your baby's first year is divided into four basic phases: phase one—*stabilization*; phase two—*extended night*; phase three—*extended day*; and phase four—*extended routine*. The focus of this chapter is on feeding times and related mealtime activities that are associated with the fourth phase, extended routine (for six months and beyond).

By six months of age, PDF babies make the transition from a four-hour, four-liquid-feedings-per-day routine to three meals a day (breakfast, lunch, and dinner), with one additional liquid feeding offered at bedtime. (By way of review, "PDF" stands for *parent-directed feeding*, an infant-management strategy designed to meet the nutritional, physical, and emotional needs of the baby, as well as the needs of the entire family. This feeding strategy is developed fully in *Babywise*.) If you are nursing, this last feeding each day is necessary to maintain your milk supply. You will supplement the three main meals with baby food. Eventually you may add an afternoon snack, when five or six hours separate lunch from dinner.

PRAYER

We believe life is more than a cosmic accident that happened without rhyme or reason. The existence of a personal, benevolent, orderly God is part of our world view. If it is part of yours, too, then consider offering a prayer of thanks at each mealtime. Parents act as substitutes for their children in several different ways. For example, we are to serve as their moral conscience until their own is fully developed. We make wise decisions on their behalf until they grow in wisdom. And we offer thanks on their behalf for the food they are about to receive. The first eternal truth your child will participate in is touching the throne of God with prayer. Pray with your children, especially at mealtime. The early establishment of healthy prayer patterns is important. Verbally giving thanks sets an example that honors God. When you pray with your child, hold his or her little hand and say, "Let's bow our heads and thank God." What a blessing it will be to have a child who at fifteen months of age voluntarily waits before he or she eats until a prayer of thanks is offered.

INTRODUCING SOLID FOODS

Parent-directed feeding continues in the pretoddler months with the addition of solid foods. Parents usually introduce solids to their babies when they are between the ages of four to six months. Your pediatrician will advise you about when to start your child on solids.

Factors influencing when to start food supplements include the baby's age, weight gain, and sleep patterns. The introduction of solids doesn't mean you should suspend liquid feedings. The calories gained from breast milk or formula are still of primary importance. Neither solid nor liquid feedings are nutritionally sufficient alone.

Getting Started

Mothers are naturally concerned about the nutritional health of their babies and often ask questions such as: "What should I feed my baby?"; "What if he doesn't like it?"; "How does feeding solids fit with her daily routine?"; and, "Where do I begin?" One guide to remember is this: Many of the common sense nutritional principles that apply to you as an adult also apply to your baby.

Initially, you should offer your baby his or her solids at the normal feeding times. For example, if you have been feeding your baby at 7:00 A.M. (breakfast), 11:00 A.M. (lunch), 3:00 P.M. (dinner), and 7:00 P.M., then solids should accompany the three major meals. Continue to offer the breast or bottle before serving solids. Your goal by the end of your child's sixth month is to align his or her mealtimes with those of the rest of the family.

Breast-feeding mothers should continue offering a minimum of four nursing periods a day in order to maintain an adequate milk supply. Begin feeding your baby with one breast. Offer the solids next, followed by the other breast. If you find that your baby is not taking the solids well, experiment by offering some solids first, then offer the breast, offer solids again, and then finish on the breast. With bottle feeding, offer half a bottle, then the solids, then the remaining contents of the bottle.

NOTE: Don't offer solids to your baby then two hours later nurse, followed two hours after that with more solids. That's snacking, not eating, and it will disrupt your child's hunger patterns and sleep/wake stabilization.

Even at mealtime, be looking for training opportunities in order to avoid retraining. Don't allow poor eating habits—such as fingers in the mouth, playing with food, and spitting out food—to become a normal pattern of your child's behavior. It only means correcting the child at a later date. To help your child become better coordinated with a spoon or fork, allow him or her to play with a spoon during bath time, not mealtime. As the child moves to more textured foods (Cheerios™, peas, bananas, and finger foods), offer the appropriate utensil. The child will naturally use whatever is easiest. Initially, this means the baby's fingers, but in time (usually by eighteen to twenty-four months), he or she will master both spoon and fork. Be patient! Learning to hold these utensils properly is a motor skill and part of the child's normal growth process.

Introducing Cereal

When introducing cereal to your baby's diet, start with *your* most convenient feeding of the day. Be patient with the process. Placing a spoon in the mouth of your four- or five-month-old not only is a new experience for you, it is equally unfamiliar to your baby. Your child will initially tongue-thrust the food right back out—not because he doesn't like it, but because he doesn't know what to do with it. Taking food from a spoon is usually mastered in three or four days.

By the second week, you can offer rice cereal at breakfast, lunch, and dinner. (Other cereal mixes, such as oatmeal, barley, or wheat, can be introduced to your baby's diet after vegetables and fruits are successfully introduced. Check with your pediatrician for the recommended timetable for adding other cereals.) Start by mixing one tablespoon of rice cereal with four to five tablespoons of breast milk or formula. Initially, the consistency will be thin, but not so thin as to run off the spoon. Gradually increase the amount of cereal to five to eight tablespoons, thickening the consistency. You can start introducing vegetables two weeks later. Because cereal is an excellent source of iron, we recommend that you continue feeding at least one serving of it a day for up to a year.

Introducing Vegetables

Your baby should receive three cereal portions a day for two weeks before starting him or her on vegetables. Each meal must be supplemented with a liquid feeding. The following *suggestions* (not *rules*) may be helpful when it's time to introduce vegetables to your baby's diet. Start with the noon meal, introducing yellow vegetables (squash and carrots) first. A couple of days later, offer a different squash. Approximately two weeks after that, introduce green vegetables (peas and beans), followed in two weeks by fruits.

Each time you introduce another food group (vegetables or fruits), start by feeding your child a couple of tablespoons of the new food, watching later for possible signs of food allergies: excessive fussiness, diarrhea, rashes, or runny nose. Meats should be the last foods offered, and you may hold off introducing meats until your baby is up to one year of age. Eventually, your baby's menu will look similar to this:

Breakfast: **Cereal and fruits**

Lunch: **Vegetables and fruits**

Dinner: **Cereal, vegetables, and fruits**

How much should each serving be? Within reason, allow your baby to set the amounts per serving. Age-appropriate amounts are usually listed on baby-food containers. If in doubt, check with your pediatrician's office for their guidelines.

Introducing Fruits

Your baby needs the nutrition that comes from vegetables. Fruits are not a substitute for them. For your convenience, mix your baby's fruit portions with his or her cereal. Be careful about the order of servings. Because fruits are naturally sweet, children prefer them to cereal or vegetables. Therefore, we suggest you offer your vegetables first, then your fruit-flavored cereal.

Making Your Own Baby Food

Preparing your own baby food is an easy, money-saving alternative to buying store-bought brands. For example, one bag of carrots (about fifty-nine cents) will yield four to six jars of prepared baby food. The average cost of store brands of the same food is forty-five cents per jar.

It's easy to prepare vegetables such as carrots, peas, green beans, yams, sweet potatoes, and butternut squash, and they freeze well. To prepare carrots, peas, and green beans, boil them in water until tender. Then puree them in a blender, adding small amounts of purified water as needed. To prepare yams, sweet potatoes, and squash, oven cook them until very soft. Remove the skin and seeds, then puree the remainder in a blender, along with purified water. When preparing large quantities for freezing, always sterilize your containers. When needed, thaw the food in your refrigerator. Incidentally, a cookbook is a good resource for baby food preparation.

Finger Foods

Highchair finger foods are just that—finger foods and not a cereal paste. The ability to self-feed depends on a child's *grasping reflex*. When your baby's thumb and forefinger grasp develops to the point that he or she can pick up Cheerios™ (this usually happens at around eight months of age), then the baby is ready for finger foods. It's interesting to watch a baby get started with self-feeding. The little fingers find a piece of food, grasp it, take it to the mouth, and then the child uses his or her whole hand to shove it in. In time, your baby will master the skill of placing food in the mouth with just the fingers. Parents may encourage finger-food eating but should also realize this is a transitional skill. It assists the child in the transition from feeding dependence to feeding independence with the aid of a utensil.

Juices

Fruit juice is a kid-friendly liquid option you can add to your baby's diet, but it is not a substitute meal. By that we mean it isn't a replacement for breast milk or formula, nor does a child need juice every day.

The introduction of juices to your baby's diet should begin at around six months of age. We recommend offering the clear juices (apple, grape, cranberry, etc.) first. After your baby's first year, you can introduce the pulpy juices (orange, grapefruit, and so on). Because of their sweetness, you should dilute the clear juices with water by 50 percent. The diluting practice can continue until the child's second birthday. At six months, start with three diluted ounces per day, and over the next six months work up to six ounces per day.

Initially, you should limit juices to mealtimes, offering them in a sippy cup but not in a bottle. In fact, we suggest you avoid offering juices from the bottle altogether. This rule of thumb obviously includes the practice of putting a child down for a nap with a bottle of juice. In a reclining position, the juice sugars can collect easily and decay baby teeth. After your child's first birthday, a juice drink makes a good snack. You can offer it when your baby wakes up after an afternoon nap, or when the child is out shopping with mom.

Snacks

Some pediatricians recommend introducing juice and finger-food snacks by the age of six months. Snacks are fun for a baby, but like anything else, balance is needed. A snack is not a second meal—don't overdo. How will you know if you're offering too many snacks? The baby's eating habits will be affected. Your child will eat poorly at the next meal or become a picky eater. If you see either happening, cut back on the amount of snacks offered or cut them out altogether. Here are a few helpful hints about snacking:

- You don't have to offer a snack every day.

- Use moderation. Don't let snacks detract from a hearty appetite.

- Don't use food to avoid conflict. It's generally not wise to attempt to influence a child's behavior by offering a snack.

- As your child stays awake longer, avoid using food as a pacifier.

- The place for snacking should be consistent—such as in an . infant seat or highchair. Avoid allowing your child to crawl or walk around the house or store with a juice drink or snack in his or her hand.

- As a general suggestion, offer snacks in the afternoon, such as right after your child wakes up from a nap.

The Finicky Eater

Like all people, your baby will show preferences in taste. But don't be too quick to say, "Oh, he doesn't like it," and offer something else. While you will occasionally give your baby what he or she likes, you must also consider what meets the needs and desires of the entire family. When age appropriate, offer your child the same foods your family normally eats.

Many finicky eaters are created, not born. As a parent, evaluate your own relationship to food. Are you overly concerned with nutritional intake? Are you yourself a picky eater? Perhaps you are a junk food connoisseur. As hard as it may be, try not to pass on any extreme preoccupation with food. Family mealtime and the kitchen table should not become a war zone; try to make meals a pleasant experience for everyone. The following are some age-graded suggestions that can help make family dining pleasant:

Under six months of age. When possible, place your baby in his or her infant seat near the dinner table. Sight and family sounds are important to the establishment of early family identity. There will be some occasions when mealtime for the rest of the family will be playpen time for the baby.

Six to twelve months (or until the child can feed himself or herself). At this age, your baby may actually eat his or her main meal of the day before the rest of the family sits down to dinner. Then, while the rest of the family enjoys their meal together, the baby can sit in the high-chair with some finger foods. Now everyone is participating, and mom gets to enjoy her meal as well.

Twelve months and older. Family mealtime should be characterized by everyone eating together. To keep the evening meal pleasant, put more concentrated effort into dealing with highchair problems at breakfast and lunch time. That doesn't mean you won't correct during dinner, but the focus on correcting inappropriate behaviors during the other meals can speed up the process of achieving dining harmony.

WEANING YOUR BABY

Weaning, by today's definition, is the process by which parents offer food supplements in place of, or in addition to, mother's milk. That process begins the moment parents give their baby formula, or when the child first tastes cereal. From that moment on, weaning occurs gradually.

From the Breast

The duration of breast-feeding has varied in the extreme from birth to fifteen years. No one can say for sure what age is ideal. For some it may be six months, for others a year. Breast-feeding for more than a year is a matter of preference, since adequate alternatives to breast milk are usually available. During biblical times, weaning took place between eighteen and twenty-four months of age; three years was more the exception than the rule.

At birth, infants depend totally on their caregivers to meet their physical needs. But they must gradually move toward independence, one small step at a time. One such step for your baby is the ability to feed himself or herself. You can start by eliminating one nursing period at a time, going three to four days before dropping the next one. That time frame allows a mom's body to make the proper reductions in milk production.

Usually the late-afternoon feeding is the easiest to drop first, since it is a busy time of day. Replace each feeding with six to eight ounces of formula or milk (depending on the child's age). Pediatricians generally recommend that parents not give their babies cows' milk until they are at least one year of age. If your baby is nine months old or older, consider going straight to a cup, rather than a bottle. The transition will be easiest if you have introduced the cup prior to weaning.

From the Bottle

When your baby is one year old, you can begin to wean him or her from the bottle. Although an infant can become very attached to the bottle, you can minimize that problem by not letting the baby hold the bottle for extended periods of time. There is a difference between drinking from a bottle and playing with it. You can start to introduce the sippy cup to your child when he or she is as young as six months of age. Becoming familiar with it early on aids the transition process.

Weaning takes time, so be patient. Begin by eliminating the bottle at one meal, then at another, and so on.

SUMMARY

Establishing good feeding/eating habits may be the easiest facet of a child's training. The more established a child's diet and eating routines are, based on parental direction and not the will of the child, the smoother the process goes.

Introducing solids to your baby's diet is part of the natural process of growth. Even with the introduction of solids, remember to train the child so as to avoid retraining later.

QUESTIONS FOR REVIEW

1. During the extended routine phase of your baby's day, how many times should you feed your baby?

(4) 3 meals + liquid feeding offered @ bedtime.

2. When should parents normally introduce solids into their baby's diet? *between 4-6 mos.*

3. What wrong feeding habits disrupt your child's hunger patterns and sleep/wake stabilization? Explain.
   allowing "snacking." offering solids then 2 hrs. later nurse, 2 hrs. later solids etc.

4. When and how should parents introduce vegetables into their baby's diet? *after baby has had 3 cereal portions per day for 2 wks. Then add a veggie (noon) wait a couple of days then try another. 2 wks later try "greens"!*

5. What should parents offer a baby first, fruits or vegetables? Explain. *Veg. because fruits are naturally sweet, & have little nutritional value.*

6. Acts of self-feeding depend on what two factors?
   grasping reflex
   grasping food + putting it to the mouth.

Chapter Four

....

Highchair
Manners

When you add them up, your baby spends many hours a week in his or her highchair. Take advantage of this time by making it an opportunity for learning. As with many aspects of child development, there are both constant and variable influences to contend with. Parents are the constant influence on moral training. Whether at mealtime, playtime, or roomtime, parents should maintain a constant level of expectation regarding their child's behavior. For example, the instructions "Do not drop your food" and "Do not touch the stereo," differ only in the nature of the activity, not in the level of parental expectation. The variable is the place or manner of offense, but the constant is the level of expectation. The "no" of the highchair should be the same as the "no" of the living room.

Parents of pretoddlers too often isolate individual acts of behavior, rather than seeing their own need to be consistent as part of the same process. Although the settings and activities vary, parents act as the constant influence to bring to each situation the consistency necessary for orderly development and growth.

When a problem occurs at mealtime, consider any other conflicts that have taken place during the day. Are they related? Is the problem tied only to food, or does the child act similarly in other settings? For example, if your son is having trouble keeping his hands where they belong while he sits in his highchair, is he also struggling with touching off-limit items in the living room? If so, the root problem is a general lack of self-control and not exclusively a mealtime weakness.

If you demand a standard at mealtime, then the same level of expectation must be in place at other times and with other activities. In the same way, if you demand compliance while in other settings but not at mealtime, confusion and frustration will result.

SELF-CONTROL TRAINING WITH HANDS

As a parent, you are an active participant in your child's advancing cognitive development (the process of learning how to put thoughts into action). It isn't wise to delay training in hope that the process will get easier later on. Dealing with a problem "later" usually means backtracking. Make this your parenting motto: *Train, don't retrain!*

Baby and mom will spend much time together at meals; for this reason, consider mealtime an opportunity to teach basic skills. For example, instruct your baby daughter in the appropriate use of her hands and her voice, and begin to teach her early table manners. A baby learns by way of instruction and restriction. On the restrictive side, don't let her help you put pureed food into her mouth with her hands—the food usually ends up all over her face and in her hair. Also, she doesn't need to hold the utensil you're using to feed her.

These are examples of simple behaviors that need to be restricted. Bad habits started early will require corrective training later.

If you have to, hold your baby's hands away from her food. Even better, teach her where to place her hands while being fed. You save yourself much trouble when your baby masters hand control. Too often, early parental training is *reactive* and restrictive, not *proactive* and directive. For example, the child who first puts his hands in his food, then in his hair, and then on his shirt receives correction from his frustrated mother. She then has to restrict the child's actions.

Restricting behavior that was once allowed makes compliance difficult. Train the child and then release him or her to freedom. Don't allow freedoms that will eventually need restraint. In the previous example, the parent isn't managing and promoting right behavior, but is instead chasing after wrong behavior.

THE IMPORTANCE OF VERBAL INSTRUCTION

You probably wonder at times how much of your instructions your baby understands. The answer? Probably more than you think. Your child is really beginning to blossom with understanding by now. Let's look at the three phases of vocabulary comprehension and mastery.

Understanding vocabulary is the first phase. That is, the child understands the meanings of words long before he or she can verbalize them. Your six-month-old will wave bye-bye or play "patty cake" when encouraged to do so by you. By eight months of age, your child has an enormous understanding of vocabulary and demonstrates this by his or her responses to instructions such as "come to mama," "sit down," "blow kisses," "hug your baby doll," "see the plane," "touch the kitty," "wave bye-bye," and so on. Your child responds out of understanding, but hasn't yet learned to speak the words he or she understands.

Speaking vocabulary is the second level of achievement, and usually develops after about twelve months of age. Your baby will begin to babble to a toy or sibling at this age. That babbling *means* something to the child. Those are word-thoughts coming out in scrambled speech.

Reading is the third level of vocabulary achievement. It begins at around the age of two-and-a-half years, when a child starts to recognize and form letters. (For an expanded explanation of language development, see Appendix A.)

Your baby is ready to learn. While patiently providing verbal instructions, show him or her exactly what you expect. For example, when you want to teach the child where to put his or her hands during mealtime, take the baby's hands and place them either on the side of the highchair tray or underneath the tray on baby's lap. You might say, "Put your hands on the side of the tray, please," while actually taking the child's hands in yours and placing them there.

The benefits associated with proper placement of hands become obvious in light of the wrong behaviors that can result when a child doesn't know how to do this. (Just one example: a child wildly splashing pureed vegetables all over Mom's dress!) Remember, training correctly from the start eliminates the need for correcting wrong behavior later. Be patient with your child, but above all, be *proactive* in the training process; proper training won't just happen.

METHODS OF DISCIPLINE

Parents are responsible for training. The word train means to initiate, get started, set the patterns, cause one to learn. The goal of pretoddler training isn't to prevent your child from exploring life, but to help him or her develop healthy behavior patterns that will enable the child to learn about life. Those patterns include paying attention, focusing, and concentrating on what he or she is doing—all fundamental skills of life. You began the process with your basic routine, and will continue in it by encouraging your child in right behavior and by correcting wrong behavior.

In the pretoddler phase of development, behaviors needing correction are initially wrong functionally but not morally. Therefore, we correct wrong patterns and encourage right patterns. Children don't naturally grow into right behavior—they are trained into it.

There will be plenty of opportunities to train while your child sits in the highchair. The right method of correction and the right amount of limitation needed to achieve your goals depend on the age of the child. Common highchair problems are controlled and amended by a combination of the following methods:

1. *Verbal reprimand.* This requires the exercise of verbal authority.

2. *Isolation in the crib.* This amounts to removing the child from an act or place of conflict and putting the child in his or her crib. Pretoddlers can very quickly learn cause-and-effect relationships. They can also learn that behavioral expectations are not negotiable.

3. *Loss of a privilege or toy.* This is a logical consequence that also works effectively. The purpose of logical consequences in pretoddler training is to reinforce your verbal instructions.

4. A light to moderate squeeze or swat to the hand. It's a fact—discomfort gets any human's attention faster than anything else. Applying moderate discomfort as a method of correction is reserved for the older, more mobile pretoddler whose hands are touching things they shouldn't be. Neither a squeeze or swat to the hand, when accompanied by a verbal reprimand, is a punishment; both are *deterrents*, attention-drawing techniques which demonstrate parental resolve. Using either of these methods for the express purpose of calling attention to a limitation will not leave your child psychologically scarred, affect the child's self-esteem, train the child to hit other children, teach the child violence, or cause the child in adulthood to abuse his or her own children. But these methods *will* encourage your child to make right decisions.

Spanking, as traditionally practiced in our society, is not an acceptable form of correction during the pretoddler phase of development. If it is to be introduced into the life of your child, it will be much later. For now, it's enough to say that the use of verbal reprimands, isolation, loss of privilege, and squeezing or swatting the hand are appropriate disciplines for the pretoddler phase. As we move through the balance of this chapter, considering the appropriate methods of pretoddler correction, keep in mind your overall objective—helping your child gain age-appropriate self-control.

Your baby's routine in the early months created a critically important foundation for the pretoddler phase. In the next six to eight months, parents should strengthen that foundation and expand on it, in order to help the child receive and process the great amount of data that bombards him or her during the socialization stage—fourteen to forty months. Much of your success during the toddler years will be a result of pretoddler training. Don't miss the critical opportunities for learning that come during the pretoddler months. The long-term results of right training are wonderful.

Common Highchair Problems

Consider the following highchair problems as opportunities for advanced training. The offenses vary (although they are related), but the methods of correction are often the same. Included in the group of common highchair violations are:

- flipping the plate;
- dropping and throwing food;
- playing with food;
- placing messy hands in the hair;
- banging on the tray;
- standing in the highchair;
- arching the back;
- spitting "raspberries";
- screaming.

These behaviors have common denominators (the highchair and mealtime); they also share a common correction. To demonstrate that, we will take up the first two problems—flipping the plate, and the intentional dropping of food from the highchair. When working to correct a new but wrong behavior or bad habit, or to prevent one from starting, remember that *wholesome correction is always consistent*. Consistency aids the learning process, especially during the pretoddler stage.

Flipping the Plate and Dropping Food from the Highchair

Parents should place finger foods directly on the highchair tray or on a plate. When finger foods are on a plate, one common and curious temptation of a child is to pick up the plate and flip it, spilling all the contents. Don't allow that to become a habit. Mealtime isn't playtime. A firm "No, do not touch your plate, only your food," is the starting point of training and correction. If you let the child play with the plate even though he or she doesn't spill the food, you have granted your child an unnecessary freedom that will only nudge him or her closer to wrong behavior and away from right behavior. There is no developmental advantage to be gained by allowing your child to play with a plate of food.

"But I don't want to stifle my child's creativity," is a commonly stated concern. You won't! Flipping food on the floor is not an act of creativity. It is wrong behavior. Creativity must be productive to be beneficial, not destructive.

Sometimes food is accidentally dropped. When that happens, guidance, not correction, is called for. But what about the intentional dropping or throwing of food from the highchair? Those actions need to be corrected. Some parents go to extremes to avoid conflict, rather than train their children in self-control. Believing that simple self-restraining behavior is too much to expect from a child, they allow behavioral freedoms that will need correcting at a later date. We refer to this as "credit card parenting." You will pay the training price in the future, but with compounded interest. Instead of training a child not to drop food, some mothers allow the behavior and minimize damage by manipulating the child's environment.

Inflating a child's vinyl swimming pool and placing it under the highchair is a good example. With this trick the child can have fun with his or her food and the kitchen floor stays clean (until the child learns to throw food outside the perimeter of the pool). Although the mother has successfully avoided conflict—temporarily—by not insisting on a standard of behavior, she has also missed a wonderful opportunity to train in self-control. With that type of environmental manipulation, no urgency exists to train a child in appropriate mealtime behavior. Such an approach usually backfires on the parent. The self-control normally learned by properly handling food is the same self-control needed for life outside of the kitchen and for guiding the child in later life. Missed training opportunities result in slower intellectual growth.

It's possible to train your child not to drop his or her food by giving immediate attention to the offense. First, correct the child verbally. Next, provide an attention-getting squeeze or swat to the hand, if necessary. Finally, isolate him or her in the crib. The child will fuss over that consequence, but when the isolation period is finished, bring him or her back to the highchair and try again. If the child persists in the behavior (and some will), mealtime may be over and naptime might begin. One thing is for certain: *Immediate and consistent consequences speed up the learning process.* In the past, educators were concerned with parents who pushed their children too fast. Today, we are concerned with parents who don't push their children enough.

The principles of correction for flipping and dropping food are the same for the rest of the highchair offenses listed earlier. For example, the child who plays with his food (mashing it needlessly), stands in his highchair, or bangs his spoon on his tray receives first a verbal reprimand, and, if need be, either a squeeze or swat to his hand (or his thigh, if he's standing in the highchair), isolation, or both. Your choices are limited at this age when it comes to corrective methods.

If the child is blowing bubbles with his food (commonly referred to as blowing "raspberries"), then lightly place your finger over the child's mouth and give a stern, "No! Keep your food in your mouth." If further correction is needed, isolation is usually the next step. You can expect your pretoddler, especially one who started with *Babywise* principles, to respond to these methods of correction with positive results.

Whining

Whining is an unacceptable form of communication that can become very annoying. It is a learned trait, not a warning of deep-seated emotional problems. At what age might whining begin? It can happen as soon as your child begins to communicate ideas. Though half-hearted at the outset and not done out of rebellion, whining will become either a bad habit or a tool of manipulation if not attended to early. The most common way parents reinforce this habit is by giving in to it.

Whining prior to fifteen months of age usually reflects a limited vocabulary. For example, if your baby wants more food, he or she may use a half-cry form of communication to ask for it. Although that is an expression of whining, it's not a protest or a challenge to authority at this stage. The good news is this: When you rightly deal with highchair whining, you are simultaneously hedging against behavioral whining that comes in the toddler and post-toddler years.

Providing an Alternative

The root of the problem at this age is not the whining, but the lack of communication alternatives. Children between eight and twelve months of age are mentally able to communicate but are not yet verbally capable of doing so.

To prevent whining and to facilitate your child's acquisition of verbal skills, start at around eight months of age to teach your infant how to communicate through sign language. It is never too early to emphasize "please" and "thank you." Remember, your child's verbal comprehension precedes his or her verbal vocabulary. You can effectively teach the following phrases: "please," "thank you," "stop," "more food," and "all done." For a discussion of how to teach your child to sign, see Appendix B.

Work on one expression at a time, taking the child's hand through the motions while saying the word. Begin with "please," adding the name of the requested item to the end. For example, "Please, more cheese," "Please, more meat," or "Please, more drink." When you sense that your child understands but refuses to say it back, use natural consequences to reinforce the correct response. If, for example, she desires more food, don't give her any until she signs "please." If she desires to get down, keep her in her chair. If you find yourself getting into a power struggle, isolate the child, rather than giving her the opportunity to challenge you directly. Here are four reasons to teach your baby to sign:

- You are teaching and reinforcing habits of self-control.
- Signing eliminates wrong communication methods by providing right modes of expression.
- Signing aids discretionary correction in the future. There will be times when you cannot easily correct your child publicly or verbally. The silence of signing, together with mom's facial expression, communicates the same intent as verbal correction.
- You are actually teaching your child a second language during a time in the child's life when he or she is most receptive to language formation.

Don't be surprised if, when you initially begin by taking your child's arm and hand to show the child what is required, you feel resistance. This display of autonomy sometimes can be clearly seen in a child as young as seven months of age. One mother shared her story with us, describing how surprised she was to take her seven-month-old baby's hand to show the baby how to make the "please" sign, and finding that she was openly resisting the mother's efforts to guide her.

"I was taken aback when she resisted and actually tried to fight me," the mother explained. "I realized this was one of the first battles that I, the mother, must win. I stayed with it, and in one week's time, my daughter was willingly and happily signing 'please' when she wanted something." "Even more amazing was the lesson I learned; my child's surrender gave way to her own happiness." The child's ability to communicate amazed both her parents and other people who came into contact with her. "Now that she is twenty months old," the mother continued, "she signs 'please,' 'thank you,' 'more,' 'all done,' 'mommy,' 'daddy,' and 'I love you.' All this in addition to her developing verbal skills."

The benefits of early sign training pays dividends in the future. Three-year-old Eric received a Valentine's Day treat from an adult friend. The red foil wrapping paper immediately attracted Eric's attention. His mom, standing behind the giver of the Valentine's Day chocolate, caught Eric's eye and discretely signed "thank you" to him. He in turn looked up at Mrs. Ezzo, his benefactor, and with a great big smile said out loud to her, "Thank you, Mrs. Ezzo." This type of discretionary signing is far superior to the constant verbal reminder parents normally give: "Eric? What do you say to Mrs. Ezzo?"

Teach your little ones to sign, but take your time, be consistent, and above all, be patient. Both parent and child will get there.

SUMMARY

Some parents see as their duty the need to make their children happy, never recognizing that this may deprive their little ones of the strength that comes from wise restrictions and loving corrections. Mealtime behavior provides opportunities for learning and growth in self-control. Don't shy away from an opportunity to train. And remember, early training establishes right patterns of behavior that help advance a child in all future activities.

QUESTIONS FOR REVIEW

1. What is the goal of pretoddler training? What is not the goal?

2. List and describe the three phases of vocabulary comprehension.

   a.

   b.

   c.

3. Please name and briefly describe the four methods of corrective discipline for pretoddlers.

   a.

   b.

   c.

   d.

4. In corrective parenting, what speeds up the learning process?

5. What is "credit card parenting"?

Chapter Five

Waketime Activities

*I*n the building process, whether it be for a physical structure or the moral fabric of a human heart, it is vital to lay the proper foundation. Unfavorable or inadequate training during the pretoddler phase of development can seriously sabotage physical and mental development. That's why the establishment of right patterns of behavior is basic to all human potential. Parents must not only give attention to *what* is imparted, but also to *how* it is imparted.

Allowing a child to grow up doing whatever the child wishes, without placing any demands or limitations on him or her which are designed to gain compliance with a reasonable set of standards, is not fair to the child. Children need guidance most in the early stages of learning, when the foundations are being laid. If parents set the right course for a child and encourage the child to stay on that course through caring parental administration, the child will be less likely to stray and more likely to progress quickly through the process of learning.

The establishment of right patterns of learning from the start plays an increasingly dominant role in the pretoddler's development. Right patterns ultimately affect the way a child manages instruction, direction, correction, limitation, freedom, and new and growing relationships. As he or she grows, the child's world develops and becomes increasingly more complex. Therefore, how a child assimilates knowledge and learns to respond to parental cues are foundational to all future growth.

DEVELOPMENTAL DEPRIVATION

The term *developmental deprivation* doesn't refer to a child's being deprived of opportunities to learn, but of the *best* opportunities to learn. To a large extent, a child's environment determines his learning patterns. We believe learning deprivation occurs when parents consider a pretoddler's or toddler's impetuous and momentary desires to be their prime source of learning. For example, allowing a child to crawl or walk around the house unhindered, without any guidelines, directions, or restrictions, represents a dubious channel of learning. Learning this way is too often accidental and outside the context of the pretoddler's developing world.

Suggested by the nonrestrictive theory of allowing a child to explore unhindered is the idea that learning through trial and error in a nonstructured environment, wherein parents merely act as *facilitators* of learning rather than *teachers* of knowledge, is a superior training method. That simply isn't so! Trial-and-error self-exploration is inferior to structured guidance with proactive teaching. Allowing trial-and-error learning to become the primary source of education, even for a pretoddler, is time-consuming, and too often the end results are far from satisfactory. Trial-and-error parenting often creates learning environments that are greater in scope than the intellectual capacities of the child, as well as fostering the development of patterns that will require retraining later.

Pretoddlers and toddlers need direction and guidance from their parents. They must learn correct, specific responses for specific situations, and then be able to transfer the concept learned to other settings. "Do not drop your food" and "Do not touch the stereo," are examples of what we mean. Those actions are different, but the desired response to both is the same—submission to parental instruction. If parents reinforce their instruction in the living room but not in the kitchen, then the child's ability to discriminate between what his parents expect and what they allow becomes clouded.

PLANNED LEARNING OPPORTUNITIES

Learning opportunities should be predominantly the result of planning, not chance. The establishment of healthy learning patterns is the result of providing the right learning environment, one in which controlled stimuli (those factors that normally call for curiosity and investigation) are part of your baby's day. To achieve this end, plan some structured time into your baby's waketime. Those opportunities will include: 1) *structured playtime alone,* 2) *time with family members,* and 3) *free playtime.*

Structured Playtime Alone

We maintain that play serves the learning process. But the spontaneous interest of pretoddlers and toddlers is not the only influence

71

on their play, since parents control to a large extent the environment in which they learn. For this reason, both structured and nonstructured learning environments are needed. Structured playtime is a specific time during the day when a child has time to play by himself or herself. It starts in the early months with the playpen and advances to roomtime. (A discussion of roomtime is found a bit later in this chapter.)

Playpen Time

Many parents use the playpen to control their child's environment for the moment, providing confinement. While that is one legitimate use for a playpen, it shouldn't be the primary function. The long-term benefits resulting from early use of the playpen will show up for years to come. By six months of age, your baby should be taking some naps in the playpen, or have slept in it while away from home. The playpen is an essential tool for your child's safety and an effective aid to your child's learning. It fosters the most basic learning skills of life: sitting, focusing, and concentrating.

Why Use a Playpen?

There are several practical benefits to be derived from the use of a playpen:

1. *It provides a safe environment.* Playpens are a safe place to put your baby when your attention must be elsewhere and it's not the baby's naptime. They can enable you to take a shower, unload groceries from the car, care for other children, and do a host of other activities—all the while knowing your child is safe.

72

2. *It doubles as a portable bed.* The playpen can serve as a portable bed, which is especially useful when visiting in another family's home. The playpen gives the baby a clean, familiar place to sleep.

3. *It offers a structured learning center.* Most important, your baby's first structured learning takes place in the playpen. The partnership a child has with the playpen establishes foundational intellectual skills. Planned daily playpen times allow little ones the opportunity to develop in many ways. Let's look at some of them.

- *Mental focusing skills.* Playpen time helps a child develop the ability to concentrate on an object or activity at hand and not be distracted constantly.

- *Sustained attention span.* You will observe how your child picks up a toy, manipulates it with his or her hand, examines it carefully, shakes it, and then revisits the process again.

- *Creativity.* Creativity is the product of boundaries, not freedom. With absolute freedom, there is no need for creative thinking or problem-solving.

- *Self-play adeptness.* This is one of the positive signs that your baby is moving from dependence to independence.

- *Orderliness.* The first step to developing orderliness is to help your child with cleanup times. Start by placing a few books in one corner, a bucket of small toys in another, or stacking other items in a neat pile. Simple statements such as "Let's put the toys in the basket," or "Help Mommy clean up," aid the process. The object is to leave the area neat, with the child participating in achieving that goal.

If the child misses structured playtime, the repertoire of skills he might otherwise attain by these activities could be seriously delayed.

When to Use the Playpen

Schedule your playpen times at approximately the same hour (or hours) each day, selecting times when your baby is fresh and alert (not before naptime, for example). Put several interesting toys within the child's reach, or put the toys in a small basket and place the basket in the playpen. Keep the toys age-appropriate, and occasionally rotate them. The child who finds a shiny blue rattle fascinating at five months of age will ignore it at ten months of age. Local libraries carry books that describe the types of toys or activities your baby is likely to be interested in at each stage of development.

We want to briefly comment on toy selection. An important aspect of selecting appropriate toys is understanding what is *not* a toy. Tools various kinds of instruments, mechanical devices, and Mommy or Daddy's private and personal property are not toys. Mommy's earrings, billfold, and lipstick in her purse (and the purse itself, for that matter) are not toys. Neither is Dad's pocket pen or his hammer. Common sense and the age of the child are sufficient to guide parents in their efforts to find appropriate toys.

If you have twins, alternate their times in the playpen. Put one child in the playpen in the morning and the other in it in the afternoon. Occasionally try putting them both in at the same time.

If your home allows for it, vary the location of the playpen from time to time. For example, during the week you might put it in the living room. Then on the weekend, place it near the sliding glass door overlooking the backyard, where the child's siblings are playing. In warm weather, take the playpen outside. You should position the playpen so that you can easily check on your child, but where your child cannot see you. It detracts from the purpose of self-focusing playtime if the child can see mom or dad. Forcing a child to, in effect, choose between creative self-play or mom sitting in the next room is not fair to the child. If you live in a small apartment, be creative. For example, you might use a portable room divider to section off part of the living room or bedroom.

The time your baby spends in the playpen will vary with age. During the first few months, your baby should have ten to twenty minutes twice a day in the playpen. By the time your baby can sit by himself or herself, you can extend playpen time to fifteen to thirty minutes twice a day. Once your baby starts to crawl, increase the time to thirty to forty-five minutes at least once a day. Between fifteen and twenty months, your child can play up to one hour either in the playpen or possibly in his or her room. These are suggested guidelines, of course. Some days your child will play for longer periods in the playpen, shorter intervals on other days.

Here we offer words of caution and encouragement. Don't overuse the playpen by leaving your baby in it for extended and unplanned periods during the day. Playpen time normally should be a planned activity, not an all-day event. As a word of encouragement, children of all ages have a love/hate relationship with boundaries. They hate boundaries simply because they are there, yet love them because of the security they provide. That's true of the playpen. If your child doesn't appear to like the playpen at first, stay with it; he or she will come to love it in time.

Starting Late

How should you introduce the playpen if it hasn't been part of your baby's day prior to this? Start with short periods of time—maybe ten minutes a day. Over the next two weeks, work up to twenty-five minutes. After a month, try thirty to forty-five minutes. There may be some crying, but the advantages gained outweigh the passing tears. With your next child, try not to wait so long to introduce the child to the benefits of time spent in a playpen.

Roomtime

At between eighteen and twenty-two months of age, you can move your baby to *roomtime*. The principles of roomtime are the same as for the playpen, but you will be using the child's room as his or her play area. You should structure and plan this time, too, into your child's day. Playing in his or her own room doesn't mean the child can do whatever he or she pleases. The child shouldn't be allowed to ransack the room, take out all available toys, or rearrange the furniture. Some supervision is necessary. Initially, a gate may be required, but your goal is to have your child play alone in the room for an extended period of time without any physical restrictions. As the child develops self-control and demonstrates responsible behavior, you can award the child freedoms.

There may be occasions when roomtime actually will be located somewhere other than in a child's bedroom, such as when the child shares a bedroom with one or more siblings and that situation makes having a consistent roomtime period in that location unpractical. Roomtime is simply playpen time with *extended boundaries*, so roomtime can be located somewhere else in the house—in a corner of the kitchen, for example. It's important to increase a child's boundaries as the child develops.

Many parents confuse roomtime with free playtime (to be discussed in a moment). Roomtime is assigned to the child. It's a time determined by mom, not the child. Mothers sometimes say to us, "My son plays in his room on his own." That's nice, but will he play in his room when mom says to? Usually the answer is no. Just because a child voluntarily plays in his room doesn't mean he is having "roomtime," as we use the term. It's one thing for a child to do what he wants when he wants to; it's another thing for him to follow a parent's direction.

Yielding to parental instruction as *standard* behavior is part of the learning structure you're attempting to establish. The self-control inherent in obedience is the same self-control that advances the child in other disciplines.

Time with Family Members

There are some obvious activities which take place during waketime that include interaction with one or more family members. It's important to enjoy your relationship with your pretoddler, but you must find the right balance between playing with your child and becoming your child's sole source of entertainment.

There is no "right" amount of time that must be devoted to family play activities. But if you find that your child clings to you, refuses to go to dad or siblings, and cries when you leave the room, it may be the result of too much playtime with mom. In this case, the child is overly dependent on the mother for entertainment and is comfortable only with her. Such a situation closes off opportunities for others to participate in the child's life. Here are some safe play activities in which all family members can participate.

- *Reading.* It's never too soon to read to your baby or to show the baby colorful picture books (especially cardboard or plastic ones that he or she can explore alone). Many children enjoy being read to long before they can understand the words. The continuous flow of sound and the changes in vocal inflections and facial expressions attract a child's attention. Nestling your child in your lap when you read further enhances this experience.

- *Bathing.* This is another activity of your baby's day when interaction takes place. You can sing to the child, tell him or her which part of the body you are washing, or just have fun splashing. However, you should make sure the splashing doesn't get out of hand. Remember, balance is the key concept in the training process. We recommend you bathe your baby and not bathe with him or her. A child may have several bath props, such as plastic toys, a cup, or a spoon, that make bathing a fun time.

- *Walking.* Taking time for a stroll outside is a great activity for the two of you. By six months of age, your baby becomes fascinated with the treasure of God's creation. A regular walk becomes a big adventure for your pretoddler, and it is healthy for you, too.

- *Touching.* A healthy influence on a child's emotional development is the type of physical touching that comes through play activities. Play is an important part of a child's growth. Touch communicates intimacy, and together, touch and play form a winning combination. Lying down on the couch, floor, or bed and blowing kisses, tickling, and physically playing with your baby are necessary components in healthy relationship formation.

Free Playtime

"Free playtime" isn't a time when you allow your baby to cruise the house looking for entertainment. Rather, it refers to planned and impromptu times when a baby plays with his or her toys at a *play center*. A play center is a small, safe area containing a basket or box of age-appropriate toys that the child can go to at will. Parents can set up play centers in the kitchen, bedroom, living room, or any convenient spot that will allow them to observe the child from a distance. Keep the majority of toys at the play center. That doesn't mean that if the play center is in the kitchen there should be no toys in the child's bedroom. It does mean, however, that toys are not left in every corner of the house for the child's convenience.

Play is important to a child. The repetition of play activities gives a child a chance to develop and consolidate the skills that a particular kind of play requires. It also affords the child an opportunity to resolve mechanical problems with his or her toys. For example, a child first finds the drawer open on the toy cash register. He shuts it but cannot figure out how to open it again. Here trial-and-error learning plays its part. Through finger manipulation and investigation, eventually the child learns the right keys to push to open the drawer. The child will use these problem-solving techniques in the toddler stage of development, if afforded sufficient and controlled opportunities in the pretoddler stage.

Another parent-directed skill is cleanup. When play is over, help your child with this task without trying to do it all for him or her. Say to your child, "Playtime is over; let's clean up. Mommy will help," or, "Let's put your toys in your play box." By directing the child to put some, if not all, of the toys back, you are defining the parameters of playtime. Those parameters include the concept that playtime is not over until all the toys are picked up. That process instills a sense of order. It also impresses on the child a sense of personal responsibility, something every society needs to survive.

In the pretoddler and early toddler months, keep the toys simple. Stacking blocks, balls, objects that can be manipulated with the hands, and colorful books are but a few examples. Play is important, and free playtime is as important as structured playpen time and roomtime. Enjoy your child and let him or her enjoy exploring the world through play.

SUMMARY

The type of behavioral adjustments a child makes in life is greatly influenced by the child's understanding of his or her environment, other people, and awareness of self. Waketime serves growth and development. But waketime activities must be organized, rather than being free-for-all experiences which fall between meals and naps. When a child receives guidance in establishing right patterns of behavior, learning is advanced.

QUESTIONS FOR REVIEW

1. What does the establishment of right learning patterns ultimately affect?

2. What is "learning deprivation"? When does it occur?

3. What is meant by the statement: "Learning opportunities should be predominantly the result of planning, not chance"?

4. What is the difference between roomtime and free playtime?

5. What is a play center?

6. Why is play important to a child?

....

Chapter Six

Some Thoughts about Discipline

Moral learning comes as a result of moral discipline. Discipline is a process of training and learning that fosters self-control and moral development. It comes from the word *disciple*—which means, "one who is a learner." Discipline is a positive word, not a punitive action.

Children are not endowed at birth with self-control, nor is your pretoddler or toddler experienced enough in life to know how to morally discipline himself or herself. Parents fulfill that role as teachers, while children are disciples who learn from them a way of life. Parents are the moral conscience of their children and must act on their children's behalf until they reach moral maturity.

When we refer to "child discipline" in this chapter, we are focusing on one thing only: *moral training*. Moral training helps a child gain self-control. Self-control in turn helps the child control his tongue and actions, handle negative emotions, and make sound judgments. Proper discipline will guide a child to a life of integrity. It also will help the child avoid offending others, encouraging him or her instead to do kind things for them. Most importantly, the positive effects of moral discipline are seen in the results: content children who have the confidence to know why right is right and wrong is wrong, and the self-control to consistently make right decisions. The reason we discipline our children is to prepare them to face any circumstance of life wisely.

CORRECTIVE DISCIPLINE AND EARLY TRAINING

The foundations of moral training are laid early in life, and the cornerstone is discipline. Getting your baby on a routine and sleeping through the night are the results of basic discipline. As your child grows, so too grows his or her need for moral guidance, encouragement, and correction.

Since the principle function of discipline is to teach morally responsible behavior, parents should educate, guide, and emphasize inner growth, personal responsibility, and self-control. These qualities lead to behavior motivated from the *heart* of the child. We educate our children by teaching them what is expected. We guide them by encouraging right behavior and discouraging wrong behavior. From those two activities inner growth and self-control are established.

Many parents consider discipline to be a means of controlling a child's actions at any given moment. It is that, but discipline is also much more. The primary objective of early discipline is to lay down a foundation upon which the next stage of development can be built. Young children learn from concrete experience, not abstract parental reasoning, so we train by instruction and reinforce compliance with encouragement and correction. Initially, you will encourage and correct your child's *actions*. In time, your focus will be his or her *heart*, wherein all the child's actions originate.

Training the Heart

For some theorists, parenting is a matter of facilitating a child's natural and impulsive way, rather than actively directing the child's moral conscience. Reactive in nature, their nondirective approach seeks to control a child's environment in hopes of making it psychologically safe. Their theory forces the conclusion that comprehensive moral training that requires moral conformity is adversarial. It *is* "adversarial" in a sense, and it needs to be. If there is no conflict stimulating growth, then there is no thinking person at the other end of your correction. Permissive parenting dehumanizes children by taking away parental governance and the conflict that provides learning opportunities children need for becoming morally independent. They become robotic, controlled by passions and impulses but not moral thought.

Babywise II discipline is not the opposite of the nondirective approach, for that approach is *extreme*—overindulgent, manipulative, and often unrealistic in its demands. Healthy discipline, the discipline style we recommend, is positively different. The primary consideration is the child's heart and intrinsic motivation, not extrinsic manipulation. There is something about the child's heart that requires a parent's attention. And what is that? The old proverb, "Foolishness is bound up in the heart of a child," is an accurate anthropologic description. It means a child is born with the propensity to defy parental leadership and foolishly tries to guide himself.

Foolishness in the heart means a child is attempting to act wise without benefit of accumulated exposure and wisdom. The job of the parent is to transform the heart from what it is to what it should be. Everything is geared toward one common goal: taking the foolishness that is naturally part of a child and replacing it with wisdom.

Childishness and Foolishness

Throughout the training process, and especially when your child moves into the toddler phase of growth, you will need to understand the distinction between the words *foolishness* and *childishness*. Foolishness is any conscious act of willful defiance. You say, "Don't touch!" but the child touches anyway. That's foolishness. In contrast, childishness is associated with innocent immaturity—the honest mistakes children make.

Please understand that a child isn't acting childish when he or she is disobedient—the child is acting foolish. And the child isn't acting foolish when he or she makes innocent mistakes but is acting childish. In both cases the child is in need of correction, but the method of correction is different because the motive of the heart is different. One is malicious defiance, the other isn't. Understanding these distinctions will be of great assistance to you throughout your parenting years.

Foolishness needs correction, but parents should not correct all foolish behavior the same way, or with the same consequence. When correcting your pretoddler, toddler, and young child, there are four factors to consider:

1. how common the particular offense is;

2. the context of the situation;

3. the child's age; and

4. the child's overall behavior.

Always consider these four factors when making a judicial decision concerning your child's behavior. As you do, you will avoid exasperating your child, at the same time providing the corrective guidance needed.

ESSENTIALS OF DISCIPLINE

Since healthy discipline tries to develop *internal* management by educating a child in moral principle, there will be times when controlled force is necessary to bring about the desired goal. Here we offer this warning: *Controlled force without moral guidance is authoritarian; guidance without sufficient controls is permissive.*

There will be many times when your child will reject or strongly oppose your reasonable instructions. What should you do? Teach the child to obey according to the character of true obedience—immediately, completely, without challenge, and without complaint. That task is not as difficult as it may appear. True obedience is often more difficult for the parent than for the child, for children only respond to parental resolve and nothing more.

Judicial parenting doesn't allow defiant behavior to be rewarded by doing nothing about it. For small faults, wisdom may dictate that you demonstrate patience or give a stern warning. But you shouldn't consider direct and willful defiance trivial. Obedience and disobedience are moral acts, not individual preferences.

By obedience, we don't mean the yielding that results from repeated threats, bribes, or manipulation of a child through the fear of losing parental love. Far worse than these methods is that of adult persuasion. You cannot govern a child by mere logic and argument. A young child doesn't possess your moral mind; he or she isn't your moral peer. To reason with a one-year-old child in the hope of bringing him or her into moral conformity is like reasoning with the wind. It's better to lead, direct, and guide with your rightful authority, rather than craftiness. You are the parent; you know best. For the sake of your child, insist on compliance.

Principles of Instruction

All training begins with parental instruction. When we consider the role of instruction in a child's life, there are a few facts and elementary principles that can serve as a guide to success throughout all of your parenting years. Following these basic guidelines can prevent stress and increase voluntary compliance; failure to comply, on the other hand, can lead to power struggles and continuous outright rebellion as your child moves into toddlerhood.

Principle One: *When you speak to your child in a way that requires an answer or an action, you should expect a response.* Children will rise to the level of expectation of their parents. Too many parents expect little and receive exactly that. We find consistently that the requirement of first-time obedience is far less of an adjustment for children than it is for their parents.

Principle Two: *Never give a command unless you intend for it to be obeyed.* When giving instructions, be sure to say exactly what you mean and mean precisely what you say. This simple principle is commonly violated. There is no better way to teach a child not to obey than to give him instructions that you have no intention of enforcing. A child quickly learns the habit of disregarding a parent's instruction if there is no resolve behind the words. Children by nature are gamblers. The absence of clear instruction encourages them to gamble that you will do nothing.

Principle Three: *Healthy discipline is always consistent.* The child who is corrected consistently when he or she fails to obey is better adjusted than the child whose discipline is inconsistent or incomplete. Consistency provides security and freedom. The child knows what is expected and what is off-limits.

In contrast, inconsistency produces insecurity, and because the boundaries are always in question, it stifles a child's learning and his or her learning potential. Consistent discipline helps the child to learn there is a moral orderliness in the world; certain behaviors will always be followed by disappointing consequences or punishment, and other behaviors will be followed by praise and encouragement.

Be consistent with your discipline! Consistency keeps you at the right point at each stage of development. Inconsistency creates too many variables for the child to handle, forcing you to do more parenting outside the funnel. (A discussion of what we mean by "parenting outside the funnel" is found in chapter 2.) When parents reduce or eliminate variables that are not age-appropriate from their child's environment, they establish right learning patterns more quickly and firmly. Order facilitates healthy growth; unlike excessive freedom, which leads to developmental confusion.

Encouraging and establishing right moral behavior in children requires consistency and clarity of instruction. Wholesome discipline is always consistent. Unless your instructions are clear and consistent, your child is at a loss to know what to do.

Principle Four: *Require eye contact when giving face-to-face instruction.* Make it a standard practice to get your child to look you in the eyes when you are speaking. Eye contact is a focusing skill and helps any child better process instructions. The child who is allowed to look around rather than at Mom or Dad as instructions are given often struggles with compliance.

Principle Five: *Understanding context prevents first-time obedience from becoming legalistic.* Unless you give due consideration to the context of the moment, you may judge your child's right actions wrongly, and you may neglect wrong actions entirely.

Reinforcing Parental Instruction

As your child becomes more mobile, he naturally will explore his growing world. Help him adjust to his expanding world gradually. Parents should neither prevent exploration nor grant absolute freedom; there is a healthy balance to be found between those two extremes. Releasing your child to freedom must be done in accordance with the responsible behavior required by those freedoms.

The living room, for example, is off-limits only to the child who doesn't have self-control over his or her hands. After the child has learned what he or she can and cannot touch, combined with the exercise of self-restraint, parents may allow the child access to the living room.

The plant resting on the fireplace hearth was off-limits to eight-month-old Whitney. Two attempts, and two no's accompanied by two swats to her hand, established Whitney's understanding that most of the living room is touchable but not the plant. She learned, retained, and imposed self-restrictions. The developmental significance of that training was that the future freedom granted her far outweighed her momentary cry of disappointment. Don't fear the use of restraint or the light to moderate squeeze or swat to the hand. When using this practice, you are not teaching your child violence, to hit other children, or that power comes in strength. You are teaching the child, concretely, the current limits of life.

People commonly wonder what a nine- or ten-month-old really can understand and how long he or she can remember. It's amazing what a trained pretoddler mind can comprehend and retain. For example, repeating an old experiment, one day Grandpa Gary while sitting on the couch showed his granddaughter, Ashley a cookie. He hid the cookie just under the edge of the cushion, then invited her to find it. She immediately went to the cushion and took the cookie. Two weeks later, she visited again. Once in the house, she went right to the cushion and looked for another cookie. She was clearly disappointed to find nothing, but everyone realized her memory was working just fine! Although memory retention is enhanced by pleasure, parents should keep in mind that it is also reinforced by *displeasure*—the type that comes when parents set and enforce needed boundaries.

Directive and Restrictive Instruction

Paralleling a child's increased mobility is his or her mental aptitude for understanding basic instructions. Not only does the child understand, he or she is capable of learning how to respond appropriately.

Parental instruction is either *directive* (telling a child what to do) or *restrictive* (telling a child what not to do). Both types require a response of immediate compliance and are achievable because of the child's ability to understand. Don't underestimate how early that skill is developed.

Directive Instructions

Directive instructions require a response. That response is trainable. Parents can start calling attention to a right response as soon as their baby begins to show signs of mobility. For example, as soon as baby Megan begins to crawl, call her, and then walk to her, pick her up, take her where you want her to go, and then verbally encourage her by saying, "Good, Megan. You're learning to obey Mama." This helps your child become accustomed to your command voice and your praise voice that accompanies the right response.

As your child becomes more mobile and you sense he or she grasps the concept of coming, then require obedience. That will be achieved by the combination of such words of encouragement as these: "Good boy, Ryan. You're obeying Mama," or by applying one of the four age-appropriate corrections.

Restrictive Instructions

Yes, a nine-month-old *Babywise* baby really can understand basic restrictive instructions. Simple commands such as "stop," "no," "do not touch," or "do not move," are usually the first restrictive commands of early parenting. To bring meaning to those words, "stop" must mean stop, "no" must mean no, "do not touch" must mean do not touch, and "do not move" must mean do not move. These four different commands have a common link—the requirement of first-time obedience. The sooner parents instill the reality of first-time obedience within the child, the fewer behavioral problems they will observe and the more freedoms the child will enjoy. Obedience is important. You should establish it early for your child's benefit.

There will be times when your child will ignore or strongly oppose your instructions. When that happens, what will you do? In chapter 4, we introduced the four age-appropriate options for reinforcing parental instructions. Those options included verbal reprimands, isolation, loss of privilege (or toy), and squeezing or swatting the hand. As your child becomes more skilled at motoring around the house, those options must be activated if you hope to gain control over your child's impulsive behavior. Children will only respond to parental resolve. What is *your* resolve?

SETTING BOUNDARIES

To set a boundary means to limit (but not abolish) a child's freedom of: movement, environment, choices, and speech. For health, safety, and moral reasons, setting boundaries denies a child access to something he or she wants or wants to do. It could be the power button on the stereo, the hair on your dog's back, the glasses on Dad's nose, or the pen in your pocket.

The purpose of limiting your child is not to curtail his or her freedom of exploration but to give the child freedom within manageable limits, according to the child's timetable of understanding. A child possessing more freedom than he or she can handle or more right of access than he or she can manage, will get into trouble. This speaks to one of the many paradoxes in development: A child cannot enjoy freedom without surrendering some of it.

Some parents are afraid to say "no" or "don't touch" to their pretoddler. "No" is not a bad word to avoid at all costs. For a pretoddler and toddler, it simply defines the necessary boundaries. The word *no* is at the furthest extreme from the word *yes*. Most of your home is an unspoken yes, but there are some items that for now must remain off-limits to your child's little hands.

The key to setting limits for your mobile pretoddler is not in controlling the child's environment (although that will be done to some extent), but is in instilling a right response to your instructions. The goal is to train the child to your voice (which includes tone and modulation), not to the object. Your voice and tone are the constant factors of correction; the various objects in the living room are the variables.

When your child reaches out to touch an item off-limits to his or her little hands, instruct with a firm "No" or "That's a no." (Whatever statement you use, use it consistently.) If the child persists, then add a meaningful squeeze or swat to the hand (and hand only), while verbally repeating, "No, you need to obey Mama." If he or she pursues it again, you have several options available. One is to repeat the swat. Swats need to count. Some reasonable discomfort is necessary. The mother who says, "I swat his hand, but he just smiles at me," obviously is not swatting hard enough to bring some mild discomfort.

If you apply the appropriate amount of discomfort and the child still returns to the object in defiance, then you should isolate him or her to a toy-free crib. The time spent in isolation will vary, based on the age of the child, the time of day, and the nature of the offense. Periods of isolation may be as short as five minutes. That will be enough time to get your point across.

Will your child begin to associate the crib with a place of punishment? Will that affect his or her naps or nighttime sleep? To both questions, the answer is, *No!* Your pretoddler is able to discriminate between times of isolation and bedtimes. The factors surrounding isolation are different from those surrounding bedtime. The hugs and kisses associated with sleeptime are noticeably absent in correction. Parental behavior is what cues the child as to what is going on, not the crib itself.

A third option is to remove the child (not the object) from the irresistible source of temptation. You might transport the child to his play center, saying, "Play here. These are Ryan's toys."

Power Struggles

Can a ten-month-old pull a parent into a power struggle? Yes Many do it every day! A power struggle results when parents fail to exercise their authority wisely. That is, they allow themselves to be forced into a "must win" situation over a seemingly minor conflict. There will be some early parent-child conflicts in which parental resolve must be victorious, but you should choose well which hill you're willing to "die" on. Wise parenting is superior to power parenting.

Here is an example of how a minor conflict can turn into a serious battle of the wills. The portable heater was off-limits to Ryan's little hands. When he touched it, he received a verbal reprimand from mom and a swat to his hand, despite the fact that the heater wasn't in use at the time. Undeterred, he began to play with it again. Once more he heard the word "No," and he received a second swat. He touched it a third time and then a fourth. Back and forth they went. Ryan's mom is by this time in a full-blown power struggle. If she gives up, Ryan learns that persistence pays off and obedience is optional. If she continues swatting him, she moves perilously close to abuse.

This is a common pretoddler scenario. There is a way to defuse the potential power struggle and maintain the integrity of your authority. Using the above example, after the second swat the mother should have isolated Ryan to his crib or bodily removed him to another room. In either case, she would have wisely exercised her parental authority and defused the power struggle. Such actions would achieve her goal without compromising her authority and without manipulating the environment.

Surrendering with Dignity

A ten-month-old should be allowed the freedom to surrender with dignity. Let's return to Ryan and the heater to demonstrate this concept. A child will often defy a parent when the parent makes the option of surrender intolerable. That is, a child will persist in wrong behavior if a parent doesn't give him or her room to surrender with dignity.

When Ryan's mom battled him toe-to-toe, her very presence made surrendering to her authority difficult, if not impossible. If she had walked away from him after her second swat and verbal reprimand, he most likely would have left the heater alone. Mom's presence extended the conflict. By leaving, she would have given him some room to surrender with dignity, rather than face a continued challenge. If she'd had to go back a third time, then removing Ryan would have been the best option. That's wisdom parenting, not power parenting. The dignity of your child, even in correction, must be preserved. Correct graciously.

Baby-proofing the House

Restricting a child's freedom in the primary rooms of your house is called "baby-proofing." That term has legitimate and illegitimate meanings. The first refers to making your home safe for your crawler and early walker. Parents need to be concerned with important safety issues. Do you have a tipsy bookcase? If so, secure it to the wall. Do you have electrical outlets overloaded with extension cords? Get rid of the danger. Make your baby's environment safe.

The illegitimate side of baby-proofing would be, for example, rearranging the entire living room so that the child is never put into a position where restrictions apply. With the exclusion of removing dangerous or priceless items, there is no need to rearrange your home; however, there is a need to train your child regarding what is appropriate and what is off-limits. When the child starts touching off-limit items, you should apply the appropriate consequences.

In general, parents who place no demands on their children have children who will take advantage of parental uncertainty and assert themselves, motivated by impulsive behavior and not moral thought. When their acts become intolerable and their parents attempt to suppress the rebellion, the children develop feelings of contempt for the parents' "softness" or inconsistency. Future behavioral problems that result from the lack of boundary-setting are usually more serious than those engendered by the opposite extreme overly strict discipline.

As a word of encouragement, parents who raise their infants by the principles of routine found in *Babywise* find that their pretoddlers have a much greater inclination to yield to parental instruction during this stage of development than children who had no routine in infancy. A child raised with immediate self-gratification early in life is less well prepared to handle the conflict that boundaries create later on—and usually the child's parents are, too.

SUMMARY

Healthy discipline consists of a number of essential principles and actions, some encouraging, some corrective. The encouraging side for the pretoddler includes affirmation, praise, and rewards. The corrective side consists of verbal reproof, allowing natural consequences to come and run their course, isolation, restrictions, loss of privileges, and discomfort to the hand. Each activity has purpose, meaning, and a legitimate place in the overall learning/training process.

QUESTIONS FOR REVIEW

1. What is the primary purpose of discipline?

2. What is the definition of the word "foolishness"? What is "childishness"?

3. Summarize the five principles of instruction.

   a.

   b.

   c.

   d.

   e.

4. The four restrictive commands of early parenting are "stop," "no," "do not touch," and "do not move." To bring complete meaning to those words, what must happen?

5. In reference to boundary-setting, what does the word "no" represent?

Chapter Seven

Nap and Sleeptime Activities

*a*s stated in *Babywise,* where there is ability there is also a natural capacity. Your baby has already demonstrated both the natural ability and the capacity to sleep through the night. Sleeping through the night is an acquired skill that results from right training. This chapter focuses on sleep-related activities for both your pretoddler and toddler. We will conclude the chapter by responding to a number of common sleep-related questions.

NAPS AND NIGHTTIME SLEEP

Unlike feeding patterns, infant sleep behavior is quite variable due to individual differences in children. Remember, stable sleep patterns are based on stable hunger patterns. When there are a number of disruptions in your baby's eating patterns, there will be corresponding changes in the baby's sleep patterns. If there are a number of disruptions of evening sleep (such as those that sometimes occur during family travel), the baby's daytime behavior can be greatly affected.

Sleep is an important part of a baby's life and will continue to be a vital aspect of your pretoddler's day and night. Children in the pre-toddler phase will not differ appreciably in the amount of time they spend sleeping. That may change in the toddler phase, but for now, continue encouraging healthy patterns of sleep.

Naptime

Naps are not an option based on your baby's desires. When nap-time comes, the baby goes down. It's that simple. For optimal devel-opment, children need daytime rest periods. A toddler's ability to take a nap depends to a large extent on the habits the child has developed in his or her first year. As a general rule, though, naps tend to fall into place naturally. Don't underestimate the importance of your baby's nap! Even when your routine changes and your baby is more wake-ful, naps are still very important.

At six months of age, the average *Babywise* baby takes two one-and-a-half to two-hour naps, plus an additional "catnap" in the late afternoon. By eight months of age, the baby will require only the morning and afternoon naptimes. That pattern continues until the child reaches approximately eighteen to twenty months. At about that age, the morning nap is dropped, leaving only the afternoon nap.

Waking Up Happy

A parent's beliefs about sleep highly influence a baby's wake-up disposition. Your baby's disposition upon waking can be happy and content when you follow three basic rules.

Rule One: *Mom, not baby, decides when the nap starts.*

Rule Two: *Mom, not baby, decides when the nap ends.*

Rule Three: *If your baby wakes up crying or cranky, it's most often because he or she has not had sufficient sleep.* The baby may have awakened due to a dirty diaper, a noisy neighbor, the beginning of sickness, or an arm or leg stuck between the crib slats.

If you leave the baby in the crib, even though the baby may fuss or cry, he or she will probably go right back to sleep (within ten minutes) for another rest period that extends thirty to forty minutes.

When your baby gets enough sleep, you will notice a happy disposition. The baby will make cooing sounds, letting you know it's time to get him or her up. Here, too, balance is important. There will be times when your pretoddler and toddler may need five minutes of comfort in mom or dad's arms as he or she adjusts from naptime to waketime. Those moments can be some of the most precious of all in your parenting.

Nighttime Sleep

At six months of age, your baby's nighttime sleep patterns are well established and an average of ten to twelve hours of continuous sleep is the norm. Those patterns will change little over the next eighteen months, with a few brief exceptions due to illness or teething.

COMMON SLEEP PROBLEMS

As we use the word "common," we do so in reference to *Babywise* babies and not babies in general. Problems commonly experienced by demand-fed babies are not experienced by babies on a routine. As you discovered with the success of *Babywise*, sleep problems for babies have much less to do with *nature* than with *nurture*.

Sleep is a natural function of the body. The primary cue that an infant needs sleep is drowsiness. Sleep cues are influenced (often negatively) by a variety of sleep-association props. Some sleep props, such as a special blanket or stuffed animal, are usually harmless, while others, such as the nighttime bottle, pacifier, and thumb sucking, can be addictive. The problem with sleep props, for the most part, isn't in getting the child to fall asleep initially; it is the difficulty of helping the child learn to get back to sleep without the prop.

The Nighttime Bottle

For the older baby, the most common sleep prop is the nighttime bottle. Too many children become conditioned to going to bed with a bottle and can't fall asleep without it. You can avoid the bottle prop problem by not ever getting into the habit of putting your child down with a bottle. That doesn't mean your baby will *never* take a bottle in the crib; there will be some naptimes when baby, bottle, and crib form a convenient alliance for a busy mom. As long as this doesn't become a habit, it won't be addictive.

Blankets

So that your child doesn't become overly attached to one blanket, consider limiting a blanket's use to the crib or bed, perhaps occasionally taking it with you on long car rides. Don't let your pretoddler drag it everywhere he or she goes. Although a common blanket provides a sense of familiarity, true security is tied to relationships, not objects.

Pacifier

There are many good reasons for using a pacifier with your newborn. But by six months of age, any need for additional nonnutritive sucking is greatly diminished. Does your child need a pacifier to fall asleep? If so, now is the time to start breaking the habit.

Experience and common sense teach that it's easier to do away with the pacifier at six months than at twelve or eighteen months of age. At six months, parents can just take it away. Yes, there probably will be some crying, but there won't be any emotional damage. If your child is older, you can prepare him a few days in advance with some encouraging words and finally a gentle "no more." Another suggestion is to pierce the pacifier with a needle, releasing the vacuum. The vacuum bubble is what makes the pacifier enjoyable; when it's gone, the pleasure is gone, often resulting in the child weaning himself or herself.

Thumb Sucking

Of the two nonnutritive sucking techniques, thumb sucking is the most difficult to control. We can take away the pacifier but not the child's fingers. As with many adult habits, parents won't be able to break the habit of thumb sucking overnight. It's a gradual process that requires consistency on the part of parents. The way you break the nighttime habit is to break the daytime habit.

If your child is between six and eighteen months of age, limit his or her thumb sucking to naps and bedtime only. When you see the thumb in the mouth, gently pull it out, saying, "Not now," then redirect the child to appropriate play.

Teething and General Sickness

Teething can disrupt nighttime sleep. When a tooth begins to break through the gum, you have the condition commonly referred to as teething. Like jaundice, teething is not a disease but a condition of growth. Your baby's first teeth will push through at between six and eight months of age. By six months, one baby out of three has one tooth; by nine months, a baby will have, on average, three teeth. Teething should not interfere with breast-feeding, since the sucking is done by the tongue and palate, not by the gums.

Discomfort, irritability, fussiness, increased salivation, and a slightly elevated temperature can accompany the eruption of a tooth. As uncomfortable as a child might seem, parents shouldn't regard teething as a catch-all excuse for chronic poor behavior or a drastic change in their baby's routine.

Obviously, teething can disrupt nighttime sleep. How can you comfort your baby and at the same time avoid establishing poor sleep habits? First, understand that the process of cutting teeth doesn't disrupt sleep in all babies (especially PDF babies). There is discomfort, but not enough to override well-established sleep patterns. Second, understand the temporary nature of the condition. Babies don't cut teeth for weeks. The norm is usually a couple of days per tooth. And there are medications that can help. Your local pharmacy has over-the-counter teething gels that serve to numb the gums. Usually the numbing is limited, so acetaminophen is commonly recommended to help the baby to relax and go to sleep.

If the problem is so serious that it does keep your baby awake, comfort the baby by rocking, but don't take the baby to bed with you or resort to nursing or feeding the baby. Sleeping with you won't make the child's gums feel better, but it *will* promote an undesirable sleep prop. Provide comfort when comfort is needed, but when those teeth finally break through, get back to your regular routine. If your child continues to wake during the night, it's not out of need but habit. The child must relearn how to fall back to sleep without your intervention—and that won't take long at all.

You can handle illnesses in a similar manner. Stay as close to your routine as possible and follow your doctor's advice regarding the use of medications. Usually a decrease in appetite will accompany an illness. Don't force your child to eat, but maintain adequate liquid intake as prescribed by your pediatrician.

Again, provide comfort when comfort is needed but avoid habit-forming practices that will require correction in the future. After an illness passes, it may take up to three days before your child accepts the reality of his old routine. So, once your child returns to health, get back to your routine.

MOVING FROM A CRIB TO A BED

Moving a child from a crib to a bed takes place in the toddler phase of development, not the pretoddler phase. The crib-to-bed transition usually occurs between eighteen and twenty-four months of age. A child who is trained to first-time obedience greatly facilitates this transition. It should be obvious that if parents don't require first-time obedience during the day, then instructions to stay in bed at night or during naps will hold no power. Going from a crib to a bed is a freedom. What will keep the child there? Only your word. The goal isn't simply to put your child in a bed, but to have the child stay there all night.

To help make the transition smooth for you and exciting for your child, try to include him or her when going out to purchase the new bed. Maybe the child can help dad set up the bed, or shop with mom to pick out his "big boy" or "big girl" sheets for the bed. Take advantage of the weekend to make the switch. Most dads will be home Saturday morning to help make a big deal out of a child's first night in his or her own bed.

Initially, don't give your child the freedom to get out of bed without your permission. After naps or in the morning, have the child call out to you before getting out of bed. Teach the child a common phrase, such as, "Up, please" or "May I get up, please?" Letting the child have verbal access to you is usually enough to keep him or her in bed.

Finally, when making the transition, buy or build a side rail for the bed. Children move around on the bed during their sleep much more than adults do. Side rails are as much for the parents' peace of mind as for the child's safety.

QUESTIONS ABOUT PRETODDLER SLEEP

Having surveyed many *Babywise* mothers and fathers, the following represent the most commonly asked questions regarding pretoddler sleep.

Our six-month-old has always slept through the night. Now, all of a sudden, he is waking and crying. Why is this happening? What should we do?

This is a fairly common problem which can occur anytime

between five and eight months of age. There are four typical reasons why babies wake at night. The first is *hunger*. The child's waking may be a signal that he is ready for solids. The second reason is associated with *no longer needing the third nap* of the day (in late afternoon). It may be time to drop the full nap and move to a catnap or no nap at all. With three full naps a day, the baby may now be getting too much sleep. The third reason for waking at night is *teething*. It's easier to identify this since daytime irritability usually accompanies the condition. The fourth reason for nighttime waking is associated with *changes in your baby's daytime routine*. Has there been a major change? Has this been a particularly busy week? Do you have relatives visiting who feel it is their responsibility to hold your baby all day? Have you just gotten back from a trip? Check your baby's routine.

Our six-month-old baby is sleeping fine at night but all of a sudden is waking forty-five minutes into each nap. Is this normal? Should we get him up?

It's not uncommon for PDF pretoddlers between five and eight months of age to begin waking halfway through their naps and give all the appearances of being ready to get up. If this begins to happen with your baby, don't get him out of bed. Instead, train him to fall back to sleep on his own. Pretoddlers need to nap longer than forty-five minutes.

This new waking phenomenon can last anywhere from three days to three weeks. The root cause appears to be associated with a new sense of alertness that accompanies the pretoddler phase of development. In *Babywise*, we discussed the alternating relaxed sleep patterns (RSP) and active sleep patterns (ASP). As your child comes out of his first relaxed sleep state, his new sense of alertness is affected by familiar sounds. It could be the sound of a door shutting, the furnace going on, the school bus outside bringing home siblings, or a host of other familiar noises. The alertness seems to trigger curiosity, and instead of falling back to sleep, he wakes and cries for you.

Your child needs to learn how to fall back to sleep and not let his curiosity control his sleep patterns. Rather, allow his sleep patterns to control his untimely curiosity. You can check to make sure everything is okay, but ultimately you need to leave him in his crib to fall back to sleep.

Unfortunately, in order to correct this situation, some crying will take place. The cry is not one of need but of desire. As you read in *Babywise*, don't respond to a baby's cry automatically, but rationally consider what is best for the baby in the long run. In this case, the continuance of excellent sleep behavior is far more important than the admittedly emotion-wrenching disturbance of your baby's cry.

Our child is now standing in her crib but doesn't know how to get back down and begins to cry. What should we do?

Standing in the crib is half of a newly acquired skill. The other half is learning how to sit down after standing. You can aid the process by taking a few minutes after each nap to show your baby how to sit down. Take her hands firmly and guide them down the crib slats, helping her sit. Over time, she will get used to the sensation of letting herself down. If you help her down every time she cries, you're only delaying the learning process. There will be no need to learn to sit if she knows that when she cries you will always come in. This is another time when no response to a cry is the best response, for the baby's sake.

Our child keeps losing his pacifier at night and begins to cry. What should we do?

A sleep prop is any device needed to help the child fall back to sleep once the child awakens. In this case, the prop is the pacifier. The more you get up and return the pacifier to the child's mouth, the more you reinforce this wrong expectation. It's probably time to wean him from it.

Our baby throws off her covers at night, gets cold, and then begins to cry. What should we do?

Children move around in their sleep (some more than others), making it difficult to keep them covered. As a parent, you only have three preventative options: dress your child warmly at night, turn up your central heating, or purchase a safe room heater. There is one caution we'd like you to consider concerning nighttime sleep and room heaters; be careful not to place your baby too close to a heater in hopes of compensating for the coldness of the night. Overheating a child can be a greater health threat than allowing her to become too cold.

My husband and I will be traveling for the next couple of weeks with our pretoddler son. How do we maintain his routine, especially when we move through other time zones?

There are two considerations to focus on when traveling: *1) training your baby to sleep other places than in his crib,* and *2) adjusting your baby's routine to each new time zone.*

In preparation for travel, begin a few weeks in advance putting your child down for his naps or nighttime sleep in the playpen. For a couple of nights, put the playpen in the living room, family room, or your bedroom. Drape the outside of the playpen on two sides with towels or extra baby blankets, then take those blankets or towels along on your trip; or borrow some towels when you arrive at your destination. The blankets or towels serve to **enclose** the child's sleep environment and reduce potential distractions.

If your trip is to an adjacent time zone, time adjustments will be fairly automatic. However, when flying through three or four time zones, make the adjustments to your baby's routine once you arrive. The type of adjustment depends on whether you are traveling east to west or west to east. With the first, you have an extended day; with the second, you have an early night. If you have an extended day, add another feeding and possibly a catnap. If you go east, split the bedtime difference in half between the old and new time zones. For example, your baby's 7:00 P.M. West Coast bedtime is equivalent to 10:00 P.M. East Coast time. Splitting the difference between the two time zones would make your baby's first East Coast bedtime 8:30 P.M. Over the next couple of days, work his bedtime back to 7:00 P.M., making as many adjustments as needed to his daytime routine.

We suggest you limit sweet drinks and snacks while traveling. A long trip is a particularly bad time to add extra sugar to your baby's diet, and extra snacks can suppress hunger to the point where it can affect digestive stabilization. Disrupting your baby's hunger metabolism often affects his sleep/wake cycles, something neither you nor your baby want to have happen while traveling. Overall, your PDF baby will be a joy to travel with, and the few problems you may encounter will be temporary.

My seven-month-old still fusses for five to ten minutes at each nap. Will he ever outgrow this?

Yes, he will. For some babies, fussing is the only way to release pent-up emotional energy. As long as he is taking good naps, that little time of fussing will soon be a thing of the past. So don't change a thing you're doing now. Just continue to be patient with your child.

SUMMARY

As your baby grows through the pretoddler and toddler phases, the amount of sleep needed will gradually decline, but the need for quality sleep will remain unchanged. The problems you might encounter in your child's sleep behavior will be minor in comparison to the giant strides you will make in sleep stabilization during this time. Your proactive mind-set for parenting, together with your common sense, will help you meet any sleep challenges that might arise.

Babywise II has taken you to a higher level of understanding of the amazing world of your baby. As you have applied the principles presented in this book, you undoubtedly have recognized that your child is now ahead in many important ways. It's okay to recognize your role in facilitating the process of your child's right development; you've done a good job. Keep up the good work!

QUESTIONS FOR REVIEW

1.   What are the three "wake up happy" rules?

a.

b.

c.

2.   By definition, what is the problem with "sleep props"?

3.   What is the one thing that will keep a child from getting out of bed?

4.   List four reasons why PDF babies begin waking up at night during the early pretoddler phase.

a.

b.

c.

d.

5.   Why do some babies wake up early from their naps? What should you do about this?

Child Language Development

*a*nyone attempting to learn a language can tell you that doing so can be a very difficult task, and it takes years to achieve any sort of fluency. However, babies come equipped with a phenomenal ability to achieve total fluency in a language in about three years, with very little practice and almost no conscious thought required. Parents are the models for a child's development, and the area of language development is no different from the many other areas of growth discussed in this book. The following are some ideas that can help encourage your child's language development.

• ***It's not necessary to use "baby talk."*** It is very tempting to reduce what you are saying to what you think your baby understands, such as, "Ryan, no touch; that bad." Children are wonderful decoders. If you say, "Ryan, don't touch that; it's bad to do that," he will (even at the young age of six months) understand the tone of voice, the facial expression, and any gestures you might use. By twelve to fourteen months, he'll understand enough of the words and intonations to figure out exactly what you are telling him. Children are wonderful imitators, too. Why not give your child a chance to learn the correct sentence structure?

• *Talk about anything and everything.* This will give your child a chance to pair words with concepts. Even though he or she will not understand all the words at first, what a great exposure to the world you are providing. When you go to the grocery store, talk about what you are buying, where you are going next, and things you see in the aisles. A pretoddler certainly doesn't understand everything, but you are laying a broad foundation for the future.

• *Read, read, read!* Reading books to your child is a wonderful way to expose the child to words and concepts. We recommend Jim Trelease's *Read-Aloud Handbook* (New York, N. Y.: Penguin Books: 1985).

• *Once your child starts speaking, expand on what he says.* For example, when you are giving your daughter a bath and she says, "Boat down," you can respond by saying, "Yes, the boat went down." This not only recognizes what your child has said, but also gives her the correct form of a full sentence. Cute though it is, you really don't want your child to start kindergarten using baby sentences!

• *Above all else, relax.* With few exceptions, children learn language in spite of anything parents do or think they have done to inhibit it!

CHILD LANGUAGE DEVELOPMENT

The following is a general outline of the stages of child language development for Ryan, the fictional baby we mentioned earlier (and for *your* child, as well!). Please remember that each child develops at his or her own rate, and the ages given are only approximate.

Birth to three months: A familiar, friendly voice comforts Ryan. He smiles at his mother or another familiar person. He has different cries for hunger, a dirty diaper, and fatigue. Ryan coos and goos.

Two to four months: Ryan begins to pay attention to the person speaking to him now, responds to an angry tone of voice by crying, and turns toward a source of sound. He laughs out loud and begins to babble, making sounds like "bababa."

Four to six months: At this age, Ryan begins to respond to his environment and understand vocal inflection and intensity of utterances. He strings together several different sounds ("badabadaba"), and he blows raspberries.

Six to nine months: Ryan now listens with greater attention to other's utterances and understands words such as "no," "bye-bye," and his name. He begins to echo sounds and actions that others make.

Nine to twelve months: He begins to follow simple directions—such as "Do not touch" and "Come here"—and shakes his head yes and no. The long-awaited first real word is uttered, and Ryan begins to "jargon"—he vocalizes strings of sounds paired with intonations, which sound like questions, statements, and demands.

Twelve to eighteen months: By this time Ryan recognizes familiar objects and people and identifies body parts. He adds more and more words to his vocabulary during this period and begins to put short sentences together.

Eighteen to twenty-four months: He correctly identifies more and more objects when asked to do so and listens to simple stories.

Don't worry if your child is a month or two late at attaining any given language skill listed above; children mature at different rates. If your child is not speaking at all by the age of two years or appears not to respond to you by the age of one year, you should ask your child's doctor for referrals to professionals who can help.

Teach Your Baby to Sign

To teach your baby to sign is to teach him or her a second language. Like all skills, time, patience, and encouragement are required for success. Start with the basics (the first four listed) and then gradually expand the child's signing vocabulary. Have fun!

PLEASE

Rub chest with hand in a circular motion.

MORE

Bring the tips of fingers together to rest on thumbs, then bring fingertips of both hands together.

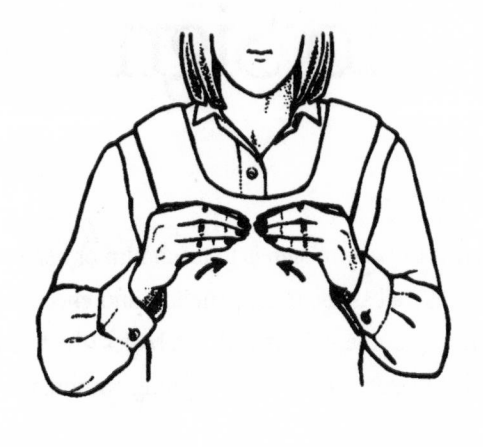

THANK YOU

Place tips of the hand (fingers together) against the mouth and throw hand forward, similar to blowing a kiss.

ALL DONE

Hold both hands with fingers spread apart, palms facing chest. Shake palms away and down.

YES

With hand in a fist, "nod" it back and forth. (Similar to nodding your head.)

NO

Bring index finger and middle finger together to rest on thumb in one "snapping" motion.

I LOVE YOU

Extend and hold thumb, index finger, and little finger with palm facing toward subject.

MOMMY

With fingers spread apart, thumb touches middle of chin.

DADDY

With fingers spread apart, thumb touches middle of forehead.

EAT

All fingertips resting on thumb, bring hand toward mouth a couple of times.

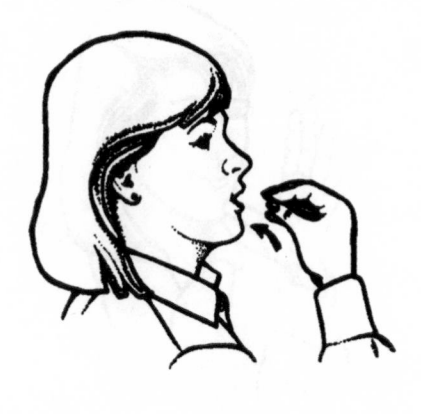

THIRSTY

Slide tip of the index finger down front of neck.

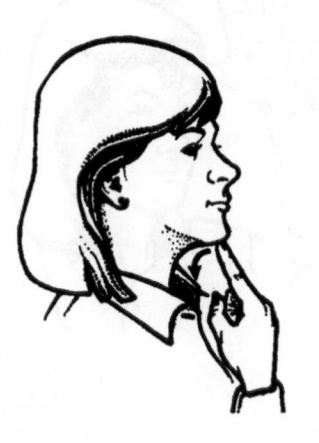

HUNGRY

With hand in the shape of a "C," place it just below the throat, palm facing in, and bring it down.

DRINK

Place your hand in the shape of a "C" in front of mouth, thumb resting on chin, and bring hand up as if pouring a drink into mouth.

STOP

Little-finger side of the right hand is brought down quickly on the left palm. (As if you were cutting something in half.)

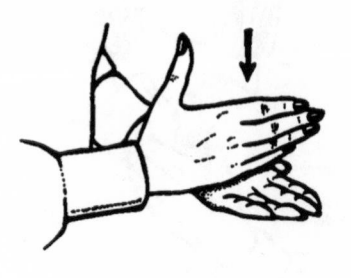

Hints on Potty Training

*a*s a society, parents have gone from toilet training starting at one year to no real training at all. Both extremes are based on specific philosophies of life—behaviorism and neo-Freudianism. As evident in other aspects of parenting, we know that a young child doesn't have the ability to always decide what is best for himself or herself, or to exhibit self-control. That's why parents, with their superior wisdom, are in control. Here are some common sense suggestions to help you when the time for potty training arrives.

Signs of Readiness

The age when a child is ready to start potty training varies from child to child, but there are a few "clues" parents can look for that will tell them when their child is ready to begin:

- At between eighteen and twenty-four months of age, you may notice your toddler staying dry during naps or for two-hour periods. In addition, the child may begin waking up either dry or nearly dry in the morning. These developments indicate that the bladder is able to hold urine for two or more hours.

- Your toddler begins to stop in the middle of play or other activities while having a bowel movement, or reports having had a bowel movement or wet diaper.

- Your toddler expresses a desire to imitate parents or siblings who are using the toilet.

Once you see these signs on a regular basis, then:

1. Purchase a potty chair and have it in the bathroom so your toddler can become familiar with it.

2. As in other areas of parenting, develop a routine.

3. Place your toddler on the potty (tell the child this is going to happen, don't ask if he or she would like to do it): a) after each meal, b) before going to bed and before naptime, and c) when waking up in the morning and after naps.

Relax, be patient, and give your child a chance. Put your toddler in training pants for naps and use diapers at night until you are confident of night dryness. Children vary in their ability to remain dry at night. You might begin right away putting your child to bed in training pants at night and see how he or she does. The majority of children day and night train within a short period of time.

Since potty training is a skill, goal incentives can be used in the training process (M&M™-type candies, raisins, or whatever is appropriate for your child). Many children become bladder-trained before they accomplish bowel control. However, once you know your child is capable of going in the potty but refuses, then you are facing a potential discipline issue. Just as when the child moves from the crib to a bed, your voice command is what should keep your child sitting on the potty chair. As a general rule, parents who have trained their child to first-time obedience have fewer problems in potty training than those parents who have not. If soiling continues to be a problem with a child who is over two-and-a-half years of age, hold the child accountable for his or her accidents. By that we mean the child should clean up himself or herself, plus the soiled clothes.

Once you start training, stay with it. False starts are confusing and they telegraph to the child your own uncertainty. The older the child becomes, the more he or she realizes you have no control over this process, and it can become a discipline issue. Again, be patient and remember that each child is unique and that the process takes time.

One final note: If your child is still on a bottle, is not on any routine during the day, is not sleeping through the night, naps inconsistently, sleeps with you, or doesn't obey instructions, then toilet training will not come easily. You must deal with those other issues first.

Subject Index